TESTING THE WATERS: LGBT PEOPLE IN THE EUROPE & EURASIA REGION

DISCLAIMER:

The views expressed in this publication do not necessarily reflect the views of the United States Agency for International Development or of the United States Government

TABLE OF CONTENTS

LIST OF TABLES

ACRONYMS AND ABBREVIATIONS

AIDS	Acquired Immune Deficiency Syndrome
CAT	Convention against Torture and Other Cruel, Inhuman or Degrading Treatment or Punishment
CDCS	Country Development Cooperation Strategies
CEDAW	Convention on the Elimination of Discrimination Against Women
CERD	Convention on the Elimination of All Forms of Racial Discrimination
CoE	Council of Europe
CRC	Convention on the Rights of the Child
CSO	Civil society organization
E&E	Europe and Eurasia region
EaP	Eastern Partnership
ECHR	European Convention on Human Rights
ECtHR	European Court of Human Rights
EIDHR	European Initiative for Democracy and Human Rights
ENPI	European Neighbourhood Policy Instrument
EU	European Union
FtM	Female to Male (transgender)
GFATM	The Global Fund to fight AIDS, Malaria and Tuberculosis
HIV	Human Immunodeficiency Virus
ICCPR	International Covenant on Civil and Political Rights
IDAHO	International Day Against Homophobia and Transphobia (May 17)
ILGA-Europe	International Lesbian, Gay, Bisexual, Trans and Intersex Association – Europe
LGB	Lesbian, gay and bisexual
LBT	Lesbian, bisexual and transgender
LGBT	Lesbian, gay, bisexual and transgender
MARP	Most At Risk Population
MSM	Men who have sex with men
MtF	Male to Female (transgender)
NGO	Non-governmental organization
NHRI	National Human Rights Institution
OSCE	Organization for Security and Cooperation in Europe
SOGI	Sexual orientation and gender identity
STI	Sexually Transmitted Infection
UN	United Nations
UNAIDS	Joint United Nations Programme on HIV/AIDS
UNDP	United Nations Development Programme
WHO	World Health Organization
WSW	Women who have sex with women

EXECUTIVE SUMMARY

As public awareness of sexual orientation and gender identity increases in the E&E region, so does the expression of hostility towards lesbian, gay, bisexual and transgender (LGBT) people in general society. Despite some recent breakthroughs, LGBT persons regularly meet with a lack of support or outright condemnation from families and communities, political and religious leaders, law enforcement, service providers (e.g., in health and education), and employers.

In recent years, awareness of and interest in LGBT issues and programming has been growing across USAID. President Obama signed a Presidential Memorandum directing "all agencies engaged abroad to ensure that U.S. diplomacy and foreign assistance promote and protect the human rights of LGBT persons" (Office of the Press Secretary, 2011). USAID's Policy Framework 2011–2015 argues that in order to deliver meaningful development results, USAID must ensure that no one's views are discounted because of their sexual orientation or gender identity. USAID's Gender Equality and Female Empowerment Policy provides a roadmap for closing gender gaps and an inclusive approach to foster equality that will be especially important to people excluded because of their sexual orientation and gender identity (USAID, 2012a). The USAID Strategy on Democracy Human Rights and Governance also notes that USAID emphasizes an inclusive development model that recognizes the rights of and opportunities for LGBT persons among other marginalized populations (USAID, 2013). Men who have sex with men and gay men are recognized as target populations for USAID's work with most-at-risk populations in the Global Health Strategic Framework (USAID 2012b).

Missions, however, may not be fully aware of the status of LGBT persons in the region or the tools available for designing programs that effectively tackle the most pressing issues. The aim of this report is to help fill the gap in knowledge and practice by deepening institutional awareness so that Mission staff can include attention to sexual orientation and gender identity matters in their work.

This report discusses the principal issues pertaining to LGBT populations in the E&E region, including: (a) a clarification of relevant terms; (b) the experiences and ability of LGBT persons to live authentic lives free from violence and discrimination; (c) public attitudes toward LGBT people; (d) discrimination and human rights violations; (e) international and national protection vehicles and their implementation; (f) LGBT non-governmental organizations (NGOs) and allies active in the region; and (g) recommendations for engaging LGBT people and addressing the needs of LGBT individuals and NGOS through USAID programming and indicators that can be used to measure success.

WELL-BEING AND THE ABILITY TO LIVE AUTHENTIC LIVES FREE FROM VIOLENCE AND DISCRIMINATION

LGBT people are continually thwarted when trying to live freely and authentically. They confront negative attitudes in their families, overt discrimination throughout society, and regular violations across the entire spectrum of their rights. It is very difficult to "come out" because of prevailing norms surrounding gender roles in the E&E region. The courage required to speak openly about one's sexual orientation and gender identity, as well as the psychological pressure of feeling forced to remain hidden from family, friends, and society leave individuals feeling isolated, vulnerable, and at risk. Negative consequences flow from this situation—individuals experience a range of psychological trauma and sometimes turn to harmful behaviors (e.g., alcoholism, drug use, or suicide) to cope. The process of coming out is a core issue for LGBT people. It is incremental and ongoing and occurs repeatedly in new situations, often placing LGBT people at risk of rejection, discrimination, or danger.

It is important to recognize that the transgender community across the E&E region is very diverse. A great many transgender people, particularly those in physical transition, are subjects of continual passive and aggressive curiosity and frequently targeted for abuse, direct discrimination, andrepudiation , as well as physical and psychological violence. Undue difficulty is often imposed on those who try to change their identity documents to reflect their gender identity, changed sex classification and names. During lengthy sex reassignment processes, people may carry documents that do not reflect their gender. The unwanted disclosure of information can severely hamper a person's ability to live, work, travel, study, and access health care.

Numerous reports from the region have identified the family home as an original source of oppression of people who are suspected of being LGBT or who have come out. Access to support mechanisms from LGBT organizations, such as information and services like counseling or peer support, appears to be virtually non-existent in rural areas, smaller cities, and towns, and very limited in the larger cities across the region. Safe spaces are not always safe owing to attacks by those who are opposed to recognizing the rights of LGBT people, but virtual spaces do offer a gathering place.

ATTITUDES TOWARD LGBT PERSONS IN THE E&E REGION

Public opinion surveys suggest that a general homophobia is the pervasive attitude, with the majority of the public appearing to have a negative opinion of LGBT people. Qualitative evidence suggests that a large majority of the population would prefer not to see visible manifestations of LGBT identity in public places – either on the streets (marches, parades, and festivals), in media or in political life. This includes not having to encounter, on a personal level, expressions of sexuality and gender that transgress social norms (e.g., personal romantic relationships). Therefore, LGBT people often remain invisible and silent in public and social life.

An adverse consequence of increased LGBT advocacy in the region is the corresponding increase in the range of vocal and visible opponents within governments, religious communities, and the general public. Owing at least in part to the influence of religious officials, the public's professed regard for LGBT people as diseased or morally deficient persists. Religious and political leaders often frame non-heterosexual sexual orientation and non-traditional gender identity as an aberration, sin, disease, perversion, or mental illness that threatens national cohesion and identity as well as religion and leads to social breakdown.

LGBT people's quest to exercise their human rights is often framed as the desire for new or special rights rather than universal human rights. Protecting children, the family unit, society's morality, and national integrity are often given as reasons for restricting the rights of LGBT people. It appears that many public figures portray the demand for recognition of LGBT rights as an existing threat to the traditional social and political balance, which requires that gender roles be assigned within social norms. The increasing visibility of LGBT people has been accompanied by an increasing number of negative portrayals in some countries, and the media is considered to be a primary transmitter of discriminatory attitudes. It appears that level of education affects whether people internalize such attitudes—people with higher levels of education tend to be more tolerant.

HUMAN RIGHTS VIOLATIONS OF LGBT PEOPLE IN THE E&E REGION

Prevailing social and political attitudes have meant that direct and indirect discrimination against LGBT populations in all sectors has become the norm throughout the region. LGBT individuals endure both abuse directed at them and services that do not account for them. Different types of discrimination are sometimes inflicted upon LGBT people at the same time because they possess the characteristics of more than one vulnerable group. For example, a person may be a lesbian mother and ethnic minority, or a transgender migrant sex worker. In general, the home, school, workplace, and "street" (outdoor, public spaces) have been identified as the primary places of discrimination. LGBT people are strongly pressured not to come out as LGBT and at times are verbally and physically attacked. Very few incidents are reported to authorities because victims fear further discrimination.

Civil and political rights violations include exclusion from public policy processes, excessive bureaucratic impediments in all areas of government when registering an NGO or obtaining event permits, including the banning of LGBT events, attacks by state and non-state actors and a lack of state protection of LGBT people even in the face of blatant homophobia and transphobia, legislative acts that ban the discussion of LGBT people and homosexuality, invasion of privacy, rape, and blackmail.

On the public level, demonstrations and events that have diverse gender identity-related content often appear to ignite violent resistance, and LGBT activists are targeted. Over the past decade, the most visible public flashpoints for overt LGBT discrimination and human rights violations in the region have been around NGOs' attempts to hold public events that highlight LGBT culture, such as diversity or equality rallies, film festivals, and Pride marches. In addition, public officials (including law enforcement) and private individuals have targeted private places such as LGBT centers and offices where LGBT people gather, as well as clubs and bars. Laws on protecting minors from "homosexual propaganda" limit public discussion and displays of materials (e.g., posters and flags) that are supportive of LGBT people.

Prevailing legal codes regarding non-discrimination that may provide a long-term means of recourse generally make little difference in the daily life of LGBT individuals, including how they interact with those who provide or affect the delivery of vital services or sources of income. Across the E&E region, country reports and testimonies show that hiding one's sexual orientation when accessing health, housing and education services is normal and appears most often to be considered necessary for employment. Education systems perpetuate negative stereotypes through curricula known to negatively characterize LGBT people and create obstacles that hamper LGBT students' learning by not addressing hostility they face from students and staff. Many transgender people (mostly MtF) turn to sex work owing to to difficultly in finding formal employment. Because of their often heightened visibility, transgender peoples' stories regarding the workplace indicate that they cannot obtain employment or eventually leave their jobs because of harassment and bullying. Health care professionals lack training and skills in delivering care to LGBT people and often exhibit discriminatory attitudes. Also, access to and delivery of health services to transgender people are serious problems across the region and reports indicate that medical gender reassignment is not easily accessible in the region.

Finally, there are no provisions for same-sex partners to be recognized as family in any E&E country. Therefore, in terms of health, benefits, tax, insurance, next of kin, and various other areas where family status is important, LGBT people cannot access rights, responsibilities and benefits equal to that of opposite-sex couples.

VEHICLES FOR THE PROTECTION OF LGBT PEOPLE'S BASIC HUMAN RIGHTS IN THE E&E REGION

E&E countries have signed a number of UN, Council of Europe, and European Union conventions and agreements that require the protection of all citizens' human rights. Reports and news articles from E&E countries indicate that a predilection toward EU membership is more influential than institutions such as the CoE at encouraging changes that protect the rights of LGBT people. Generally, LGBT people are often unable to seek redress or protection because anti-discrimination laws, hate crime legislation, and related policies are uniformly weak or non-existent. Across the region, there is little evidence of the political will to adopt and enforce legislative and policy measures that combat discrimination or mandate tolerance of LGBT persons. Failure to recognize discrimination and crime based on sexual orientation or gender identity is widespread, and there is little effort to ensure that victims can obtain justice. Much recent human rights advocacy has been directed toward the inclusion of protection for LGBT people in non-discrimination legislation. Albania and Montenegro are the only E&E countries that currently have comprehensive non-discrimination laws that include sexual orientation and gender identity. Other than in non-discrimination legislation, the prohibition of sexual orientation and gender identity (SOGI) discrimination is codified in only a handful of laws in the region. With regards to the legal recognition of gender identity, where the right to gender reassignment exists in the E&E region, it is with the proviso of an initial diagnosis of Gender Dysphoria (Gender Identity Disorder is the term currently used in the region) and subsequent compulsory sterilization and compulsory divorce if married.

National Human Rights Institutions are the primary state institutions responsible for protecting LGBT people's human rights when they are violated by public authorities or if authorities do not take action when rights are violated by other parties. Law enforcement and judicial officials responsible for enforcing the rule of law in the region appear to discriminate against LGBT people by not upholding the rule of law and carrying out justice. Across the region, LGBT people report that instead of being protected, they are subjected to further traumatization when reporting discrimination or crimes to the authorities. While there appears to be a growing trend of police acting professionally and aiding LGBT rights-related civil society events, the same cannot be said about police performance when LGBT people are attacked or harassed while living their daily lives.

CAPACITY OF NGOS TO ADDRESS LGBT CONCERNS

LGBT NGOs exist in all E&E countries. No study has been conducted of LGBT NGOs to determine their capacity, but reports indicate that, while they are active, they face many challenges and are often small, only sometimes registered, and rarely have many full-time staff or large budgets. While formal registration of these civil society organizations (CSOs) may be difficult in most E&E countries, it is allowed. Across the region, LGBT human rights defenders face ever-present challenges: a lack of existing data on LGBT people, political repression, and a lack of supportive allies, as well as an increased safety risk in some places. In addition, it is often beyond the capacity of existing LGBT NGOs and CSOs to work on a larger scale because they do not have the necessary financial resources or technical capacity to do so.

Regional-level NGOs include international NGOs and coalitions. They engage with international organizations and send representatives to international conferences. They advocate for national and local LGBT NGOs and provide support via training and financial assistance. Forming partnerships with allies and networks is particularly important for LGBT NGOs in the region, as they allow organizations to find common ground and learn about each other's issues. In terms of advocacy, allies help legitimize claims, develop skills and access networks that interface with state bodies. Allies include donors and partners who work in areas such as gender issues, HIV/AIDS, and human rights.

RECOMMENDATIONS

The scale of the work needed to address the challenges facing LGBT people cannot be underestimated. The path forward for USAID likely requires internal policies and guidance on addressing issues important to LGBT people and integrating them into USAID programming. Facilitating more rigorous research, data collection, and well-informed program design can help USAID and implementing partners engage LGBT people and NGOS and the challenges they face. Evidence-based policymaking and programming begins with research into the difficulties facing USAID LGBT programming.

Obstacles to implementing LGBT programming cluster around: (1) the possibility of violent reactions, and (2) the intransigence of those who do no not wish for LGBT people to fully exercise their human rights. Also, LGBT people are often hard to reach because they fear exposure to hostile elements in society.

Specific recommendations include:

- Strengthen USAID knowledge and capacity for LGBT engagement, which includes developing USAID-generated guidance and building USAID/Washington and Mission staff's knowledge of LGBT people, NGOs, and methods for engaging them in the E&E region.

- Increase the integration of LGBT perspectives in the design of projects and strategies by identifying and empowering LGBT champions, including analysis of LGBT issues in Country Development Cooperation Strategy (CDCS) and project-level analysis, and researching and developing indicators to be used in monitoring and evaluation.

- Create opportunities for sustained engagement with LGBT NGOs and activists by orienting them to USAID and creating standing LGBT working groups.

- Build LGBT NGOs' capacity as civil society actors by undertaking organizational capacity development activities, encouraging the diversification of funding sources, providing training in more rigorous data collection methods, facilitating alliance building, and supporting the development of community cohesion.

- Support LGBT NGOs' efforts to advocate for change and protect human rights by strengthening civil society organizations' capability to advocate as well as plan, monitor, and evaluate their activities.

- Include LGBT people and NGOs in other USAID programming by engaging them in advisory roles at all stages of the program cycle and including them as beneficiaries or as partners in other USAID programming. Implementers could work with LGBT NGOs to ensure their projects are responsive to LGBT people's needs. Awareness raising work and training could also benefit from LGBT outreach workers and facilitators while work in education could profit from the advice of LGBT teachers and activists when developing relevant curricula.

I. INTRODUCTION

Discrimination and stigmatization against lesbian, gay, bisexual, and transgender (LGBT) people and violation of their human rights occur in all countries in the E&E region. As public awareness of sexual orientation and gender identity increases, so does the open expression of hostility towards LGBT people in society. Despite recent breakthroughs, LGBT persons regularly experience a lack of support or outright condemnation from families, communities, political and religious leaders, law enforcement, health and education service providers, and employers. They are strongly pressured not to "come out" as LGBT and are sometimes verbally and physically attacked. LGBT people are often unable to seek redress or protection because anti-discrimination laws, hate crime legislation, and related policies are weak or non-existent in the countries in which they reside or work.[1] Where they do exist, such laws and policies most often focus on women and ethnic minorities.

LGBT non-governmental organizations (NGOs) work mainly in three arenas to address discrimination and guarantee the rights of LGBT people: (a) charting and acting on states' human rights obligations and violations; (b) strengthening LGBT community cohesion and overall organizational capacity; and (c) raising awareness of LGBT issues in various policy contexts and among the general public. Throughout the region, however, LGBT human rights defenders face constant challenges: a lack of data on LGBT people, political repression, few or no allies, and increased safety risks. Existing LGBT NGOs in the E&E region are unable to scale up their work because they do not have the necessary financial resources or technical capacity.

SCOPE OF THE REPORT

In recent years, awareness of and interest in LGBT issues and programming has been growing across USAID. President Obama signed a Presidential Memorandum directing "all agencies engaged abroad to ensure that U.S. diplomacy and foreign assistance promote and protect the human rights of LGBT persons" (Office of the Press Secretary, 2011). USAID's Policy Framework 2011–2015 thus argues that to deliver meaningful development results, USAID must ensure that no one's views are discounted because of his or her sexual orientation or gender identity. USAID's Gender Equality and Female Empowerment Policy provides a roadmap for closing gender gaps and an inclusive approach to foster equality that will be especially important to people excluded because of their sexual orientation and gender identity (USAID, 2012a). The USAID Strategy on Democracy, Human Rights and Governance also notes that USAID emphasizes an inclusive development model that recognizes the rights of and opportunities for LGBT persons among other marginalized populations (USAID, 2013). Men who have sex with men and gay men are recognized as target populations for USAID's work with most-at-risk populations in the Global Health Strategic Framework (USAID 2012b).

Missions, however, may not be fully aware of the status of LGBT persons in the region or of the tools available for designing programs that effectively tackle the most pressing issues. The aim of this report is to help fill the gap in knowledge and practice by deepening institutional awareness so that Mission staff can include attention to sexual orientation and gender identity matters in their work.

The report has three goals. First, it will describe the status of lesbian, gay, bisexual, and transgender (LGBT) persons across the E&E region, with a focus on their well-being and ability to realize their human rights and live authentic lives, free from violence and discrimination. Second, it suggests concrete ways to better incorporate LGBT people into USAID programming. Third, it presents concrete possibilities for integrated or stand-alone programming that reduces the inequalities and discrimination facing LGBT people.

The primary target audience for this report is E&E Mission and USAID/Washington technical and program office personnel who are interested in designing activities that address the experience of LGBT persons in the E&E region and staff who are carrying out gender analyses in the context of strategy development or project design. The report should also be of interest to other bureaus at USAID; other U.S. Government agencies; and USAID partners, consultants, and project implementers.

---

1. Those countries who wish to accede to the European Union (EU) will need to align their policies and laws with EU requirements for such protections.

Following this Introduction, the report discusses the principal issues pertaining to LGBT populations in the E&E region, including: (a) a clarification of relevant terms; (b) the experiences and ability of LGBT persons to live authentic lives free from violence and discrimination; (c) public attitudes toward LGBT people; (d) discrimination and human rights violations; (e) international and national protection vehicles and their implementation; (f) LGBT NGOs and allies active in the region; and (g) recommendations for engaging LGBT people and addressing the needs of LGBT individuals and NGOs through USAID programming.

REPORT LIMITATIONS

Limited data are available from international organizations. Most recent information on LGBT people in E&E countries has come from publications produced by organizations such as the International Lesbian and Gay Association-Europe Division (ILGA-Europe), the Council of Europe (CoE), Human Rights Watch, and the Danish Institute for Human Rights. USAID and other donors have not published many reports or studies and little information has been produced via social science research. Reports based on the Organization for Security and Co-operation in Europe, Office for Democratic Institutions and Human Rights (OSCE/ODIHR) database on tolerance and non-discrimination indicate that while governments do not keep track of bias crimes or incidents directed at LGBT people, NGOs are able to provide some information (OSCE/ODIHR, n.d.a). Data have been collected using small surveys of LGBT people to learn about their experiences and opinion surveys that look into public attitudes toward LGBT people. Gallup Europe, for example, which regularly surveys public opinion in Bosnia and Herzegovina, Kosovo, Montenegro, Republic of Macedonia, and Serbia, has produced annual data on attitudes toward LGBT people. The Levada Center and Public Opinion Foundation surveyed Russian public opinion, and IPSOS Strategic Marketing surveyed Montenegrin public opinion. References to sexual orientation and gender identity (SOGI) in general or LGBT people in particular have been virtually absent from available USAID documentation.[2]

The availability of robust, empirical data from local organizations is uneven. LGBT NGOs in the region collect a limited amount of data on LGBT people. Reports generated by LGBT NGOs often employed non-rigorous data collection methodologies. Anecdotal evidence from several individuals is often presented to tell the stories of LGBT people and illustrate situations and trends in that country. Comparability across countries is limited because there is little standardization of research questions or data collection instrument designs for surveys or interview protocols, either within a country or across the region. Belarus and Kosovo appear to have the least information available. For example, with the exception of Marija Savić's, *Invisible LGBT: Report on the position of LGBT community in Kosovo*, it appears that no one has produced any situation reports on LGBT people in Kosovo.

Existing LGBT research from the region tends to focus on general information about LGBT people's life experiences. Sample sizes tend to be low (n=200 or fewer), with exceptions in Russia (Kochetkov and Kirichenko, 2008), Serbia (GSA, 2009) and Ukraine (Nash Mir, 2007 and 2011a). Generally speaking, the quantitative data from samples presented in existing reports across the E&E region tend to over-represent gay men, underrepresent lesbians, and scarcely represent transgender people. This raises the issue of whether the results merit the label LGBT; it also raises questions within the LGBT community about the claims that the NGOs for which the research was conducted speak on behalf of the whole LGBT community. Only two country reports from the region—Ukraine (Ivantchenko, 2010) and Russia (Kirichenko, 2011)—focus on presenting the situation of transgender people. In comparison to other areas of social research, such as gender or disability, significant gaps exist in the standard of data collection instruments for and about LGBT people. *Nash Mir*, Ukraine (Our World Gay and Lesbian Center) currently appears to be a leader in the region in using surveys that facilitate longitudinal analysis (for example, Nash Mir, 2011).

This report uses the data provided to depict the situation of LGBT people and NGOs in the region. Although the report draws together a multitude of resources and perspectives, the findings of the report should not be considered definitive as more rigorous research is needed.

---

2. A few reports contain analysis of qualitative data related to HIV/AIDS and men who have sex with men (MSM), including an assessment identifying data gaps and needed programs for addressing HIV/AIDS among MSM (AIDSTAR 2, 2010) and gender assessments for Georgia and Armenia (Duban & Chkheidze, 2010; Duban, 2010). The gender assessments for Armenia and Serbia briefly discuss qualitative data on the media's role in perpetuating homophobia and intolerance (Duban & Chkheidze, 2010; Cozzarelli, 2010). The gender assessment for USAID Kosovo discusses the challenges faced by LGBT people (Cozzarelli, 2012).

II. RELEVANT TERMINOLOGY

Language is the basic medium of shared meaning—and can be a vehicle for repression and inclusion. This section comprises the acceptable and standardized language currently employed by international LGBT advocates and allies, including many in E&E countries.

Gender. "The socially defined set of roles, rights, responsibilities, entitlements, and obligations of females and males in societies. The social definitions of what it means to be female or male vary among cultures and change over time" (USAID, 2012a).[3]

Sexual orientation. Each person's capacity for profound emotional, affectional, and sexual attraction to, and intimate and sexual relations with, individuals of a different gender or the same gender or more than one gender (ICJ, 2007). In national and international dialogue, the term sexual orientation is increasingly being used instead of the word homosexuality in legal, political and activist contexts. However, at this time in the E&E region, the word homosexuality is still regularly used in policy contexts, and by LGBT NGOs, civil society organizations (CSOs), and activists.

Gender identity. "An individual's internal, personal sense of being male or female" (USAID, 2012a). This may or may not correspond with the sex assigned at birth, including the personal sense of the body. This may involve, if freely chosen, modification of bodily appearance or function by medical, surgical, or other means, and other expressions of gender, including dress, speech, and mannerisms (ICJ, 2007).

KEY TERM: SEXUAL ORIENTATION AND GENDER IDENTITY (SOGI)

SOGI is a key term used in international human rights forums, including both the United Nations (UN) and the European Union (EU). It unites the terms **sexual orientation** and **gender identity** in order to denote a status requiring protection in the same way that race, sex, ethnicity, religion or gender are used.

SOGI encompasses the rich variance of sexual and gender diversity found around the world. When linked in a single expression, sexual orientation and gender identity have legal and sociological similarities and differences. Both terms share concerns about a person's body and how the person's right to identify, express, or behave within that body is legitimized, outlawed, or otherwise regarded by society and by the law.

Individually and collectively, people act, express, or identify their sexual orientations and gender identities differently, based on their potential vulnerability to discrimination, stigmatization, exclusion, violations of their bodily integrity, invasion of their privacy, and the potential legal repercussions, if and when their sexual orientations or gender identities becomes visible and known by others. People also consider the relative rigidity of gender roles and norms of gender expression, the availability or absence of a supportive community, and laws that affect recognition and protection of basic human rights for both statuses.

Gender expression. "[The] way in which a person acts to communicate gender within a given culture; for example, in terms of clothing, communication patterns and interests. A person's gender expression may or may not be consistent with socially prescribed gender roles, and may or may not reflect his or her gender identity" (APA, 2008).

Sex. "The classification of people as male or female. At birth, infants are assigned a sex based on a combination of bodily characteristics including: chromosomes, hormones, internal reproductive organs and genitalia" (USAID, 2012a).

Sex markers or gender markers. Indicators of a person's sex, including honorifics such as Mr., Mrs., Miss, Ms., or Mz. In some regional languages, gender is indicated by the declension of subjects, objects, and verbs in sentence construction. Visual markers include clothes, jewelry or hairstyles that are commonly associated with a particular sex.

---

3. It was 2011 before this understanding became codified in European law in the Council of Europe Convention on preventing and combating violence against women and domestic violence (CoE, 2011c). This issue remains contentious in international forums. Participants in the 45th session of the UN Commission on Population and Development in April 2012, for example, while addressing the theme of Youth and Adolescents, looked at documents on demographic trends and aspects of their transition to adulthood, including family formation, sexual and reproductive health, gender equality, and education and workforce participation (UN Commission on Population and Development, 2012). Various countries, including Russia, decried usage of the word *gender* and challenged or did not accept language to do with *sexual orientation* in the meeting's outcome document (Hermann, 2012).

Gender dysphoria. A state of emotional stress over one's gender and a feeling of disconnection between one's assigned and perceived genders, experienced by people who believe they were born the wrong sex. Individuals are averse to some or all of the expected physical characteristics or social roles based on biological sex (Task Force on Gender Identity and Gender Variance, 2009). *Gender Dysphoria* has replaced *Gender Identity Disorder* (GID) in the fifth edition of the *Diagnostic and Statistical Manual of Mental Disorders*, published by the American Psychiatric Association in May 2013 (American Psychiatric Association, 2013). It remains to be seen how this change will be adopted in the E&E region.

LGBT. The inclusive acronym sometimes appears as LGBTI[4] or LGBTIQ and frequently as GLBT in the U.S. The term—used globally and shared by activists, advocates, and human rights defenders and their allies in the E&E region—indicates a multiplicity of identity descriptors for a category of individuals and groups who claim sexual and political identities based primarily on their same-sex practices or their challenge to gender norms. It encompasses sexual orientation and gender identity, as well as the expression of both. LGBT is a collective concept that has been claimed to assert and demand recognition as well as space and rights such as legal personhood. The term has been successfully used for political, social, and economic organizing purposes. It is worth noting, however, that the acronym LGBT is usually not present in any international or regional agreements, standards, or laws because it refers to identities rather than status. This is appropriate because laws or conventions dealing with discrimination on the basis of race or religion, for example, do not specify particular races or religions. Instead they make it illegal to discriminate against any person because of race or religious beliefs. Many of the international conventions and agreements relevant to LGBT people use terms such as other status, marginalized groups, or vulnerable populations that may or may not indicate SOGI (see above).

Lesbian. Women who are emotionally, affectionally, and sexually attracted to women. The term is used by those who self-identify as lesbian and also to denote group identity, in speaking, for example, about the lesbian movement.

Gay. Men who are emotionally, affectionally, and sexually attracted to men. The term is used by those who self-identify as gay and as a marker of group identity, in speaking, for example, of the gay rights lobby. It is sometimes also used as shorthand to encompass all LGBT people. In the U.S. and Europe, including the E&E region, for example, the word gay is commonly used as a quick and easy way to refer to Gay rights, gay Pride, and gay marriage, are all terms frequently used by political leaders, the media, the public, and by LGBT activists themselves concerning same-sex subjects. A report by the Ukrainian LGBT NGO, *Nash Mir*, for example, is titled *Gay Rights are Human Rights* (Nash Mir, 2005). As LGBT visibility increases in the E&E region, however, increasing numbers of activists are becoming aware that the word gay—which refers to the sexual orientation and identity of men, not women, bisexuals, or transgender people who do not identify as gay men—obscures consciousness of lesbian, bisexual, and transgender issues in the public mind. It is thus generally considered a best practice to avoid using the word gay as a short form of LGBT or SOGI.

The LGBT categorization has limitations. It groups women, men, and transgender people together in an attempt to recognize common marginalities, even though the discrimination individuals commonly face may be significantly different and arise for multiple reasons. For example, a Roma lesbian could experience multiple acts of discrimination because of her ethnicity, gender, and sexual orientation. The term LGBT is one lens on an individual's and a community's identity, but should not be used in ways that risk minimizing differences of history, geography, and politics, or other characteristics for which individuals face stigma and discrimination, such as their race, ethnicity, age, migration status, health status, and language. For some, the term LGBT may be understood and questioned as a Western construct (Global Rights Initiative, 2008), though the limited survey data available show that this is not a uniform opinion in all countries in the region (Human Rights Action, 2009). Interestingly, activists are willing to attest to hearing the term LGBT as a Western term (K. Sabir, personal communication, 19 March 2012).

---

4. As consciousness of the social, legal, and human rights situations of intersex populations is currently increasing, the acronym LGBTI is increasingly employed by global and national advocates. The "I" stands for intersex. Intersex has similarities but also has unique legal and medical distinctions from those of transgender (Task Force on Gender Identity and Gender Variance, 2009). A significant proportion of international and national LGBT advocacy organizations now refer to LGBTI to describe their work, as consciousness of the social, legal and human rights situations of intersex populations is currently increasing. However, this report does not include intersex issues in its scope, as specific intersex advocacy appears not to be reported on in the E&E region at this time. In Bosnia and Herzegovina and Serbia the acronym LGBTIQ is frequently used: here "Q" can stand for both Queer or Questioning. See the section on relevant terminology.

Bisexual. Men and women who are emotionally, affectionally, and sexually attracted to both men and women.

Transgender. An inclusive term (frequently shortened to "trans") for people who experience and/or express their gender differently from the social norms attached to their birth-assigned gender; it is an umbrella term that includes people who are transsexual, cross-dressers or otherwise gender non-conforming (USAID, forthcoming). "The term may include but is not limited to: transsexuals, cross-dressers and other gender-variant people.

Transgender people may identify as female-to-male (FtM) or male-to-female (MtF)" (GLAAD, n.d.). The community also includes people whose gender expression or identity do not fit neatly into the categories of male or female. There appears to be a common false assumption across the E&E region that transgender people seek to express sexuality, as opposed to gender, by dressing, behaving and speaking as they do. The word transgender does not imply particular sexual orientation. Transgender people may be straight (heterosexual), lesbian, gay, bisexual, or asexual, just as non-transgender people can be (Global Rights Initiative, 2008).

Transsexual. Individuals who feel a profound discord between their gender identity and the sex they were assigned at birth. These individuals may or may not choose to modify their bodily appearance or engage in medical gender reassignment processes (Personal communication,[5] Kohler, R., Trans-Europe, September 29, 2013).

Cisgender or Cis. Individuals whose perception and expression of their gender match the sex they were assigned at birth--people who are not transgender. This relatively new term challenges notions of normativity by affirming that we all have a gender identity, and all are equally normal (Schilt & Westbrook, 2009).

Asexual. An asexual person is a person who does not experience sexual attraction. Someone who is asexual may experiencelove and non-sexual attraction. "Asexual people have the same emotional needs as anyone else, and like in the sexual community we vary widely in how we fulfill those needs. Some asexual people are happier on their own, others are happiest with a group of close friends. Other asexual people have a desire to form more intimate romantic relationships, and will date and seek long-term partnerships. Asexual people are just as likely to date sexual people as we are to date each other" (The Asexual Visibility & Education Network, n.d.)

Intersex. A person who is born with characteristics (mostly gonadic, chromosomal, or genital) that do not seem to fit the typical definitions of female or male reproductive and sexual anatomy. Intersex anatomy may or may not show up at birth. The term hermaphrodite was used historically, but is considered inappropriate in common parlance (Global Rights Initiative, 2008).

Queer. A range of sexual orientations and gender identities that include lesbian, gay, bisexual, and transgender that is generally used in the context of identity politics. In parts of the world where queer was once used as a derogatory term, some LGBT people have assimilated the word and employed it as a more appropriate and inclusive term than gay.

Questioning (Q). A sexual identity, often transitional, that transgresses heteronormativity (defined below) in which people neither view or identify themselves as heterosexuals, nor socially, politically, or culturally as LGBT, because they are examining and defining their sexual or gender identities.

Homosexuality. Sexual, romantic, or affectional attraction to a person of the same sex. The term is widely found in laws and common parlance of LGBT NGOs, CSOs, and activists. It has been superseded by the term sexual orientation. At one time, legal codes in the E&E region criminalized homosexuality specifically with regard to male same-sex relations, while female same-sex relations appear to have been largely overlooked (GAP, n.d.). [6]

Heterosexuality. Sexual, affectional, and emotional attraction to people of the opposite sex. Heterosexual people are also referred to as straight.

Men who have sex with men (MSM) and women who have sex with women (WSW). These terms concern sexual conduct between same-sex people. They do not imply gay or lesbian identities or emotional

---

5. This personal communication was with Cary Johnson.

6. Although it is no longer usually used to denote legailty, some regional Russian anti-homosexual propaganda laws specifically include homosexual or homosexualism as well as "bisexualism and transgenderism [sic]," for example, those in Samara (Chechurina, 2012), Kaliningrad (New Kaliningrad, 2013), Bashkortostan (Republic of Bashkortostan, 2012), and St. Petersburg (Administration of Saint Petersburg, 2012).

attraction. In the E&E region, as elsewhere around the world, public health strategies, policies, and programming focused on tackling and treating HIV and AIDS use the terms MSM and WSW, rather than referencing social or political identity descriptors such as LGBT (UNAIDS, 2011).

Heteronormativity. A set of norms that considers heterosexual identity and traditionally gendered behavior to be the standard. Sexual attraction, behavior, or gender expression outside of this norm meets with various levels of disapproval and marginalization by society. Heteronormativity is maintained through social and cultural norms and legal regulations.

Homophobia. "A psychological term originally developed by Weinberg (1973) to define an irrational hatred, anxiety, and/or fear of homosexuality. More recently, homophobia is a term used to describe the fear, discomfort, intolerance, or hatred of homosexuality or same sex attraction in others and in oneself (internalized homophobia)" (Forshee, n.d.).

Transphobia. "A fear, disgust, stereotyping, or hatred of transgender, transsexual, and other gender non-traditional individuals because of their perceived gender identity, expression, or status" (Forshee, n.d.).

Sexual rights.

> Human rights that are already recognized in national laws, international human rights documents and other consensus statements. They include the right of all persons, free of coercion, discrimination and violence, to: the highest attainable standard of sexual health, including access to sexual and reproductive healthcare services; seek, receive and impart information related to sexuality; sexuality education; respect for bodily integrity; choose their partner; decide to be sexually active or not; consensual sexual relations; consensual marriage; decide whether or not, and when, to have children, and pursue a satisfying, safe and pleasurable sexual life. (Collumbien, et al., 2012)

Coming out. The process of initially revealing and acknowledging one's deeply felt or suspected sexual orientation or gender identity to close intimate friends or family. The term also captures the disclosure of one's sexual orientation in heteronormative environments. This process is usually viewed as a stressful and risky, but potentially liberating experience. Being "out" generally refers to clearly expressing one's sexual orientation or gender identity openly in any environment. LGBT people may experience coming out over and over in life, as they move into different jobs, cities, and social environments.

Outing. The intentional or accidental disclosure of one's sexual orientation or gender identity to others by a third party without one's consent.

Hate crime or bias crime. Criminal acts such as intimidation, threats, property damage, assault, or murder committed with bias as a motive. The terms "hate crime" and "bias crime" pinpoint the reason for committing a type of crime, rather than a specific offense within a penal code. Where it is included in the criminal code, the motive may result in harsher punishment when a court decides penalties, but in the E&E region, the term describes a concept rather than an actual legal definition (OSCE/ODIHR, 2009).

Ally. "A person who is a member of the dominant or majority group who works to end oppression in his or her personal and professional life through support of, and as an advocate for, the oppressed population" (Washington & Evans, 1991).

LGBT human rights defender. LGBT activists who advocate for and defend LGBT people to ensure that their human rights are protected and upheld. These activists risk aggression and human rights violations such as harassment, incarceration, torture, or murder (Eguren & Caraj, 2010).

III. WELL-BEING AND THE ABILITY TO LIVE AUTHENTIC LIVES FREE FROM VIOLENCE AND DISCRIMINATION

This section describes their experiences living freely and authentically in largely unaccepting societies, and exercising their human rights in line with international human rights standards and laws.

A. THE EXPERIENCES OF LESBIAN, GAY, BISEXUAL, AND TRANSGENDER PEOPLE

COMING OUT AND VISIBILITY

There are significant social pressures for women and men in E&E countries to accept traditional gender roles (Somach, 2011). In such an environment, the act of initially coming out can be extraordinarily challenging for individuals. Many LGBT individuals never do come out due to fear of discrimination and social exclusion (ILGA-Europe, 2011d). The courage required to speak openly about one's sexual orientation and gender identity, as well as the psychological pressure of feeling forced to remain hidden from family, friends, and society leave individuals feeling isolated, vulnerable, and at risk. For some, this pressure leads them to experience severe stress, self-hatred, and depression, or to engage in harmful behaviors such as risky sex, alcohol and drug addiction, and suicide (Kochetkov & Kirichenko, 2008; Nash Mir, 2005). It also appears that revealing one's sexual orientation while in prison or while serving in the police or army (men are conscripted in Albania, Armenia, Azerbaijan, Belarus, Georgia, Moldova, Russia, and Ukraine) can be highly dangerous (van der Veur, 2007; Carroll & Quinn, 2009).

According to local activists, older Roma women, generally poor and under-educated, who are not heterosexual experience great difficulty in Serbia owing to customary expectations that limit women (talking about sexuality is not a sanctioned behavior) and norms that require constant physical contact with their families. Older lesbian Roma women lack role models, and the technology to find and contact others like them. Younger Roma women are able to behave a little differently since they are more likely to have mobile phones with internet—these are their "windows in the world" (personal communication, Mladjenovic, L., 2013 June 18)

The process of coming out is a core issue for LGBT people. It is incremental and ongoing; it can take some people decades. Over time, most LGBT people move from self-doubt to self-acceptance, with many stages in between (Ivantchenko, 2010). For LGBT people who are already out and simply trying to live fully and freely, coming out happens again every time they mention or refer to their LGBT Identity in an unfamiliar context or to a new person. In the E&E region, an LGBT person's public disclosure that challenges traditional gender roles places that person at risk of rejection, discrimination, or danger.

FAMILY VIOLENCE

Even though there are no studies in the region on LGBT community and domestic violence, research conducted elsewhere has identified two key areas of concern. First, LGBT youth are more likely to suffer violence by their own families when they are suspected or revealed to be LGBT, especially transgender youth (Stieglitz, 2009; Stotzer, 2010). Moreover, the level of resilience of transgender youth is associated with family support, so rejection by the family increases the likelihood of depression and suicidality. The Parliamentary Assembly of the Council of Europe has recognized the "significant human rights dimension" of the social exclusion of LGBT youth that puts them at a higher risk of drug abuse, depression, and suicidality when compared to heterosexual youth (Takács, 2006, Council of Europe Parliamentary Assembly 2008).

The available statistical data on coming out in the E&E region are very sparse. The data in the table below appear to be from very small surveys on the environments in which LGB people come out and to whom they come out. These surveys do not appear to have included transgender populations.

7

Country	Not out %	Out to friends %	Out to family %	Out at work %	Out to everyone %	Out at school or university %
Albania (GISH, 2005) N= 87 individuals (3 women, 84 men)		10	9	7		
Armenia (Carroll & Quinn, 2009) N=130 GBT	35.3	43.8*	2.5∞		18.4	7
N= 70 LBT	20	60*	3∞		17	
Bosnia and Herzegovina (Durkovic, 2008) N=210 #	2.4	26.7	26.2^ 23.8~	24.8	81.4	24.8
Georgia (Quinn, 2007) 120 respondents		33.3	13.3			
Russia (Kochetkov & Kirichenko, 2008) 3,800 respondents				17		

Notes: * Close friends, ∞Out only to family, ^ Nuclear family, ~ Extended family
The statistics provided indicate those who answered "yes" and exclude those who answered with "some." Also, 65-69 percent of survey respondents did not answer the questions related specifically to family, friends and work.

THE UNIQUE EXPERIENCE OF TRANSGENDER PEOPLE

Transgender people face a number of problems that are specific to their gender identities and not their sexual orientations, including heightened levels of violence, lack of access to appropriate and timely healthcare (including, but by no means limited to, sex reassignment), and obstacles to official registration of gender identity on state documentation.

It is clear that transgender people are generally targeted for abuse and discrimination in the E&E region. It is important to recognize that the transgender community across the E&E region is very diverse. It includes pre-operative and post-operative transsexual persons, as well as people who do not have access to gender modification procedures and those who do not wish to undergo such procedures (Ivantchenko, 2010; K. Sabir, 19 March 2012).

SAFE SPACES

Numerous reports from the region have identified the family home as an original source of oppression of people who are suspected of being LGBT or who have come out. Fear of "losing family honor" or wish to "avoid social shame" leads family members to shun or try to force a LGBT child or sibling to deny, hide, or obscure his or her sexual orientation or gender identity. Coercive measures include confinement in the home; ostracism (e.g., being made to use separate dishes and cutlery); expulsion from the home; forced marriage; and threat of or actual incarceration in mental institutions (GSA, 2009; Carroll and Quinn, 2009; Natsvlishvili & Aghdgomelashvili, 2012; Pink News, 2012c). Although extreme rejection and psychological and physical violence in the context of family privacy are frequently discussed in the LGBT community, it appears that very few cases are reported to authorities. In order to live full and free lives, many LGBT people migrate from villages and towns to larger cities, often exposing themselves to financial poverty and isolation. If it is possible, some emigrate to escape family and community oppression (COWI & DIHR, 2010f; COWI & DIHR, 2010i; Durkovic, 2008; GISH, 2006).

Access to support mechanisms from LGBT organizations, such as information and services like counseling or peer support, appears to be virtually non-existent in rural areas, smaller cities, and towns, and very limited in the larger cities across the region. Some NGOs, however, are able to provide physical centers that offer protection and a place to convene, or web sites that provide safe virtual gathering spaces. The literature notes that restaurants, bars, and clubs also serve as gathering places, although safety is not always guaranteed (U.S. Department of State, 2011; COWI & DIHR, 2010c).

Asylum. There is little information on LGBT people coming to or leaving the region in order to obtain asylum. While reports hint that transgender people have left the region, it is difficult to verify who left or their reason for leaving. There are examples of individuals coming to Ukraine for protection and examples of individuals from Georgia, Republic of Macedonia, Moldova, Montenegro, and Serbia seeking protection in the U.S. or Europe, but information on these requests is not readily accessible (COWI & DIHR, 2010e; COWI & DIHR, 2010g; COWI & DIHR, 2010k). (See Appendix 4b for more information).

B. ATTITUDES TOWARD LGBT PERSONS IN THE E&E REGION

Across the E&E region, terms used in in private, public, religious, and political discourse which refer to diverse sexual orientation and gender identity are generally derogatory and simplistic. By framing people only in terms of their sexual functions, opponents of sexual and gender diversity negate the essential humanity and *lived experience*[7] of the people they target. This section describes the public attitudes expressed directly to LGBT people that are reflected in the print media and public opinion surveys, using language drawn from these resources.

LGBT people are frequently categorized and stereotyped as sick, abnormal, evil, or dangerous to the nation's cohesion. The attitude of a Macedonian parliamentarian, quoted in 2010, captures a viewpoint that appears repeatedly in reports on public attitudes from across the region, "Gay people are sick people and we need to cure them instead of protecting them with law" (COWI & DIHR, 2010f). (See Table 2 below for more information on public attitudes toward LGBT people.) When judging LGBT people, opponents often associate all manner of extreme and grievous behavior with them.

> On May 8, [2012] unidentified people threw a homemade bomb at DIY, a Yerevan bar frequented by LGBT and women's rights activists. Graffiti identified LGBT people as targets. Deputy Speaker of Parliament Eduard Sharmazanov called the attack 'right and justified'" (Human Rights Watch, 2013, p. 395).
>
> *"When I heard him—whoever he is, gay or lesbian—talking about dictatorship, I thought—it's better to be a dictator than gay."*
>
> –Alexander Lukashenko, 2012 (Russia Today, 2012)

In the E&E region, the suffixes *-ist* or *-ism* are frequently added to a number of words: "homosexualist," "lesbianism," or "transgenderism." This usage implies that LGBT people are somehow psychologically or emotionally disordered or that being LGBT is an ideological choice motivated by a political or social agenda. Prior to decriminalization of homosexuality throughout the region during the post-Soviet era, these expressions were common. In Armenia, Ukraine, and some regions of Russia, homosexualist is used in connection with HIV/AIDS work (Carroll and Quinn, 2009; Personal communications: K. Andonovski, 9 April 2012; K. Kirichenko, 26 March 2012; M. Hovsepyan, 22 April 2012).

There is a wide range of offensive terms common to the region used to refer to LGBT people. (See Appendix 1 for a discussion of these terms). These terms are often heard in public settings and are even used by political or religious leaders.

PUBLIC OPINION AND ATTITUDES

Across the E&E region, traditional roles and expectations for both male and female genders are deeply ingrained (Somach, 2011). In understanding the strength of reaction against LGBT people and their claims for rights, the issue of fulfilling expectations related to gender expression—how individuals fit the roles and presentation (the behavior and appearance traditionally ascribed to each gender)—cannot be underestimated.

The majority of the public appears to have a negative opinion of LGBT people.[8] Qualitative data gathered on interactions with the general public suggest that a large majority of the population would prefer not to see visible manifestations of diverse SOGI[9] in the media, in political life, or in public places—on the streets, in marches, parades, and festivals. This preference includes not having to personally encounter expressions of sexuality and gender that transgress social norms, such as personal romantic relationships. Therefore, LGBT people often

---

7. *Lived experience* refers to the cognitive framework through which a person views the world and the context in which each person interprets his or her life experiences.

8. It is difficult to compare existing data sets on public attitudes to SOGI and LGBT people across the E&E region because the research instruments were usually built to purpose in each location and did not collect the same data or use the same data collection methods.

9. Diverse SOGI includes lesbian, gay, bisexual, transgender, intersex, asexual, gender non-conforming people.

remain invisible and silent in public and social life. For example, Russian and Serbian surveys documented public opinion on whether sexual minorities should hide their sexual orientation: 53 percent of 1,500 respondents in Russia (Public Opinion Foundation, 2006) and 45 percent of 1,405 respondents in Serbia agreed with the statement "I have nothing against homosexuals, as long as they keep their activities private" (GSA, 2009). The available quantitative data on public opinion suggest that homophobia[10] is the pervasive attitude. In 2011, The Caucasus Barometer asked respondents the question, "Do you think homosexuality can be justified?" The majority of all respondents (male and female) in all age groups said no (CRRC, 2011).[11] An annual Gallup survey in Europe, which collects the most robust and quality-controlled data in the region (Table 2), found that while opinions of LGBT people have improved slightly, wide-ranging intolerance is still the norm. (See Appendix 2 for additional information from other E&E countries).

Homophobia is shown overtly. LGBT people are openly treated with disrespect, subjected to violence, and even regarded as untouchable (PINK Armenia, 2011c). In Serbia, for example, a baseline survey carried out in 2009 with 741 young male students aged 15–19 in the cities of Belgrade and Prokuplje for the Young Men Initiative for Prevention of Gender-Based Violence in Western Balkans showed that in the three months before the survey, 19.4 percent of the total sample had verbally abused or made threats towards a man they thought was gay or feminine, and 12.7 percent had hit or beaten someone who fit that description (Care & ICRW, 2010). The same survey conducted in Bosnia and Herzegovina with 1,208 male students, found that 13.1 percent of the respondents in Banja Luka and 12.7 percent of the respondents in Sarajevo had participated in similar actions (Care & ICRW, 2009).

DRIVERS OF PUBLIC OPINION
Institutional and organized opposition. An adverse consequence of increased LGBT advocacy in the region is the corresponding increase in the range of vocal and visible opponents within governments, religious communities, and the general public. Statements made by government officials in opposition to equal rights for LGBT people have been reported in all E&E countries (U.S. Department of State, 2010; U.S. Department of State, 2011; GSA, 2009). The statements vary from condemnation to virulent hate speech. However, formal statements of support for the rights of all citizens have not equaled an end to government opposition. Government officials often deny permit requests for events, fail to speak out against discrimination and harassment, and make negative and intolerant statements about homosexuality (U.S. Department of State, 2010; U.S. Department of State, 2011). In several instances governments acquiesced to religious pressure to not allow SOGI-based rights or LGBT people to hold events, even those that did not require permits (COWI & DIHR, 2010f; COWI & DIHR, 2010g; COWI & DIHR, 2010i; COWI & DIHR, 2010k).

TABLE 2. PUBLIC ATTITUDES TOWARD LGBT PEOPLE IN EUROPE

Country	Sample size	Homosexual Relations Wrong* %	Equal rights for Homosexuals* %	Homosexual acts morally are wrong* %	Homosexuals should not show their sexual preference in public* %	The city or area where you live is not a good place for gay or lesbian people %
Albania 2012	1029	68.6	26.2	85.1		80.1
Albania 2011	1006	57.3	34.1	78.6	50.6	73.2
Albania 2010	1000	54.2	44.4	78.7	56.1	71.8

10. See http://www.pcc.edu/resources/illumination/documents/homophobia-transphobia.pdf for a very good exploration of homophobia and transphobia.

11. Ninety-six percent of 2,365 respondents in Armenia, 87 percent of 1,482 respondents in Azerbaijan, and 88 percent of 2,287 respondents in Georgia answered that homosexuality can never be justified.

10

Country	Sample size	Homosexual Relations Wrong* %	Equal rights for Homosexuals* %	Homosexual acts morally are wrong* %	Homosexuals should not show their sexual preference in public* %	The city or area where you live is not a good place for gay or lesbian people %
Bosnia and Herzegovina 2012	2426	72.0	28.2	83.0		75.1
Bosnia and Herzegovina 2011	1009	63.8	36.9	82.8	77.3	77.9
Bosnia and Herzegovina 2010	1000	74.3	27.2	89.3	76.5	74.8
Kosovo 2012	1024	81.3	33.2	92.5		81.1
Kosovo 2011	1047	74.8	27.0	90.6	69.8	71.9
Kosovo 2010	1017	64.9	28.3	90.9	48.9	71.4
Macedonia, Rep. of 2012	1025	63.6	27.6	74.8		66.6
Macedonia, Rep. of 2011	1018	65.0	28.3	81.3	66.9	64.9
Macedonia, Rep. of 2010	1000	69.4	29.7	82.8	65.8	78.1
Montenegro 2012	1000	70.7	24.2	80.2		70.0
Montenegro 2011	1000	74.9	40.1	84.1	75.8	68.1
Montenegro 2010	1000	65.8	33.1	82.5	68.8	67.9
Serbia 2012	1023	70.2	33.8	80.1		61.9
Serbia 2011	1001	71.5	43.9	80.3	80.7	59.8
Serbia 2010	1000	75.1	35.8	82.2	82.5	63.9

*Includes agree and strongly agree. Source: Gallup Balkan Monitor, 2012

Traditional churches have gained significant influence in public affairs since the early 1990s and are increasingly able to shape attitudes about gender roles and expression (Kochetkov and Kirichenko, 2008; Nash Mir, 2011; GSA, 2010). Some religious leaders contribute to the view that LGBT people are diseased or morally deficient, and their discriminatory attitudes and responses towards LGBT people can be virulent. Politicians and government officials cite religious guidance when discussing the application of anti-discrimination laws to LGBT people (COWI & DIHR, 2010h; COWI & DIHR 2010e; GenderDoc-M, 2011c; Helsinki Committee for Human Rights in Serbia, 2010; Kravtsova, 2013; Stakic, 2011).

Moldovan ordinance to protect traditional values

"Considering particular importance and historic role of the Moldovan Orthodox Church as a state-establishing institute of the Republic of Moldova; considering traditional values of Moldovan society; incompatibility with modern democratic standards of aggressive intrusion of sexual behaviour forms on the majority, which are characteristic for the most insignificant part of population; bearing responsibility for security (including ethical and moral one) of Bălți city residents"

–City Council of Bălți (Venice Commission, 2013).

Perceptions of traditional values and "new rights." Human rights related to SOGI are often combatively framed as "new" or "special" rights, rather than as universal human rights. In order to not protect such rights, leaders and policy-makers marginalize SOGI issues as exclusively sexual and fetishistic, and therefore private and beyond the scope of legal recognition. To further negate them, they frame SOGI rights as Western or European notions and deny their own indigenous LGBT populations (Bortnik, V., 2011; Stakic, 2011; GenderDoc-M, 2011c; Savic, 2013).

Protecting society's morality is a common rationalization of the restriction of LGBT peoples' rights in the E&E region. The subtext of the claim is that promoting and protecting LGBT peoples' rights leads to the destruction or corrosion of what is considered to be the traditional family unit. It appears that many public figures portray the demand for recognition of LGBT rights as a threat to the traditional social and political balance, which requires that gender norms align with social norms. The right to express non-heterosexual sexual orientation or gender identity is not perceived as having a place within that moral and social framework. For example, the debate preceding adoption of Armenia's new law on Equal Rights and Equal Opportunities for Men and Women focused on the definition of gender and the use of term. In particular, vocal opponents to the law felt that it would be used to undermine the traditional family and promote homosexuality (Muradyan, 2013). Conservative groups, pop culture personalities and religious figures joined in the reaction, which resulted in an amendment to the law which replaced the word gender with men and women.[12]

Religious and political authorities' attitudes contribute to the climate of hostility towards LGBT people and their human rights defenders. On the public level, demonstrations and events that have homosexuality-related content are often met with organized resistance targeting LGBT activists.[13] For example, events to mark the International Day Against Homophobia and Transphobia (IDAHO) in Georgia in 2012 and Montenegro in 2011 were marred by such violence, and both events had to be cancelled (Global Voices, 2012; Intergroup on LGBT Rights, 2011). Appendix 4 compiles examples of human rights violations in the E&E region.

Often, the more prolific and organized groups that oppose LGBT people, such as Love Against Homosexualism in Ukraine, Obraz in Serbia, and skinhead factions in Russia and Serbia, are tacitly supported by Christian and Muslim religious institutions (A. Maymulakhin, personal communication, 11 March 2012). These groups are often rightwing, extremist, ultra-nationalist, or neo-Nazi organizations, include elements of clerical fascism, and are generally also xenophobic and male-dominated (GSA, 2010; Kochetkov & Kirichenko, 2008; Nash Mir, 2013; U.S. Department of State, 2012).

Media. Evidence from the early 2000s indicates almost universally negative portrayals of LGBT people in print, broadcast, and electronic media. These involve negative stereotypes of varying degrees of severity, from the comedic to the serious, that include abnormality, mental illness, sexualization, and representations of LGBT people as criminals (MDI, 2006; CoE, 2011a; GISH, 2006). Reports from LGBT organizations in the region since the mid-2000s attest to the continuing negative portrayal of LGBT people, though many also point to slowly increasing visibility and increasingly neutral or supportive coverage of LGBT people in the media.

Increasing visibility, however, has been accompanied by increased negative portrayals of LGBT people in Georgia (Natsvlishvili & Aghdgomelashvili, 2012), Moldova (Soros Foundation-Moldova, 2011), Serbia (Labris, 2009), and Ukraine (Zinchenkov, et al., 2011). The media have been described as the primary promoters of societal homophobia in Bosnia and Herzegovina and Russia (Durkovic, 2008; Kochetkov and Kirichenko, 2008) and identified as contributors in Kosovo because LGBT people have been labeled as mentally ill (U.S. Department of State, 2010). Generally, LGBT people are rarely the source of the information that is aired about them, though when they are, gay men are the most frequently represented, while lesbians and transgender people remain largely invisible. (See Appendix 3 for additional information.)

Education. Survey research in Armenia, Russia, Moldova, Montenegro, Serbia, and Ukraine suggests that people with higher levels of education tend to be less inclined to hold negative attitudes that regard homosexuality as a

---

12. For a summary of the controversy and the drafting and amending of the law as well as links to related articles, see Martirosyan, 2013.

13. Please note that this paper does not use the term gender-based violence (GBV) to refer to violence against LGBT people. This is because interviewees and references did not use the term to refer to violent attacks on LGBT people. Although these attacks fit the GBV model, they appear not to be conceived of or analyzed as such on the ground.

perversion, aberration, abnormality, or as commonly described in the region—"against nature" (Pink Armenia, 2011c; Kochetkov and Kirichenko, 2008; Nash Mir, 2007; Soros Foundation-Moldova, 2011; Human Rights Action, 2009; Vukovic, Colovic, & Mojsilovic, 2008).

C. HUMAN RIGHTS VIOLATIONS OF LGBT PEOPLE IN THE E&E REGION

FORMS OF DISCRIMINATION IN THE E&E REGION
Discrimination is any unequal treatment of individuals or a group because they possess certain characteristics and the denial of or obstruction of their access to the range of state or private resources that are available to all others, including protection under the law. Three forms of discrimination are:

- **Direct discrimination** occurs when a person treats individuals or a group of persons less favorably for a reason related to one or more personal protected characteristics (e.g., age, religion, disability, race, ethnicity) in comparison with people who do not have those characteristics.
- **Indirect discrimination** occurs when an enacted provision, criterion, or practice applicable to all individuals puts persons having a protected status or characteristic at an unjustifiable and disproportionate disadvantage compared with other persons.
- **Multiple discrimination** occurs when a person is subjected to discrimination on more than one ground (such as age, disability, race, and ethnicity) in separate or simultaneous occasions (ENAR, 2011).

Prevailing social and political attitudes have meant that direct and indirect discrimination against LGBT populations in all sectors has become the norm throughout the region. LGBT individuals endure both abuse directed at them and services that do not account for them. Thomas Hammarberg, the Council of Europe Commissioner for Human Rights,[14] has focused particular attention on discrimination against transgender people as one of the most vulnerable groups in Europe, calling it a clearly "bleak situation [that] calls for urgent measures" (CoE, 2009).

Different types of discrimination are sometimes inflicted upon LGBT people at the same time because they possess the characteristics of more than one vulnerable group. For example, a person may be a lesbian mother and ethnic minority, or a transgender migrant sex worker. Although it is not officially measured and addressed through policy measures in the E&E region, multiple discrimination can and does leave individuals in extreme isolation exposed to human rights violations. Although there has been little research on LGBT people who are ethnic minorities, indications are that LGBT Roma experience discrimination in Kosovo, Republic of Macedonia, and Serbia (COWI & DIHR, 2010f; Kreuzahler, N. et al., 2012). According to COWI & DIHR (2010f), LGBT Roma in the Republic of Macedonia have faced discrimination in the LGBT community because of their ethnicity.

VIOLATIONS OF FUNDAMENTAL FREEDOMS
In general, the home, school, workplace, and "street" (outdoor, public spaces) have been identified as the primary places of discrimination (G&D, ILGA Europe & Global Rights, 2009; Carroll and Quinn, 2009; Quinn, 2007; GenderDoc-M 2011a; Durkovic, 2008; WISG, 2012; GSA, 2011). Appendix 3 offers a glimpse of the types of offenses inflicted upon LGBT people in four E&E countries. Appendix 4 includes qualitative data on the impacts of discriminatory behavior towards LGBT people from reports by LGBT organizations (c.f. Labris, 2010; van der Veur, 2007; Ivantchenko, 2010).

Recorded violations include harassment, intimidation, and violence:

- Exclusion from public policy processes.
- Excessive bureaucratic impediments in all areas of government when registering an NGO or obtaining event permits, including the banning of LGBT events.
- Attacks by state and non-state actors and a lack of state protection of LGBT people even in the face of blatant homophobia and transphobia.
- Legislative acts that ban LGBT advocacy as promoting homosexual propaganda among minors.

---

14. Of all E&E countries, only Belarus and Kosovo are not members of the Council of Europe.

- Invasion of privacy, including inappropriate data sharing and denial of changes to identification documentation for transgender people.
- Forced marriage.
- Rape.
- Blackmail, harassment, and use of improper procedures by police to arrest and detain LGBT people.
- Lack of state prosecution of those who commit violent acts.

The ongoing general exclusion of LGBT people from access to public policy processes (e.g., parliamentary decision making) that are germane to the issues directly affecting them can be seen as a form of homophobia as well as a human rights violation. In order to obtain a voice, activists and human rights defenders utilize different strategies which include public events, lobbying, and advocacy.

Freedom of assembly, association, and expression. These freedoms are pivotal in combating discrimination, enhancing communication, supporting dialogue, and improving societal understanding of issues pertaining to the human rights of LGBT people (CoE, 2011a). While there are extant LGBT NGOs in all of the countries in the region and formal registration is allowed, reports indicate that it may be difficult. Registration of LGBT NGOs is prohibited in Belarus (Bortnik, 2011).[15] The activities of LGBT NGOs are often limited. Over the past decade, the most visible public flashpoints for overt human rights violation have been around attempts to hold public events highlighting LGBT culture, such as diversity or equality rallies, film festivals, and Pride marches. Impediments are frequently raised to stop or hamper the organization of an event and the event itself.

Pride parades in particular receive much attention from opponents of LGBT people's rights. Where permit applications for Pride marches or cultural events have been submitted, official governmental impediments appear at the earliest stages of attempts to organize and include not recognizing organizing committees; refusing to grant permits on grounds of traffic disturbance, security concerns, and lack of police resources; allegations of promoting indecent morals to minors; and other procedural difficulties and irregularities (ILGA-Europe, 2006). Permissions were denied to event organizers in Belarus, Moldova, Russia, and Serbia (U.S. Department of State, 2012; U.S. Department of State, 2011).[16]

Despite bans by local authorities, activists in several countries have attempted to launch Pride parades with some degree of publicity, but the events have been dangerous owing to the lack of a security guarantee from local governments and law enforcement.[17] High-profile, violent incidents occurred in Moscow in 2006, 2007, and 2011 (Human Rights Watch, 2006; Levy, 2007; Mobasherat, 2011), and in Belgrade in 2010. In both cases, police protection was inadequate and LGBT participants were arrested. In Belgrade, around 5,000 police officers were on duty for the 2010 Pride march in order to quell rioters (Tanner, 2010).

In various ways and to varying degrees, police reactions—ranging from damage, destruction, or confiscation of materials to attacks on participants—have disrupted other types of events such as rallies, film festivals, and cultural and literary gatherings. In 2007, for example, the Council of Europe "All Equal, All Different" campaign, which highlighted social diversity and included an LGBT presence, had to cancel events in Ukraine, Moldova, and Georgia in response to extremely negative reactions from church leaders and the media (GenderDoc-M, et al, 2009, COWI & DIHR, 2010k, Natsvlishvili & Aghdgomelashvili, 2012). Appendix 4 lists many other examples.

---

15. This was gleaned from a review of all of the reports issued by COWI and The Danish Institute for Human Rights (DIHR) that summarize reports of discrimination based on sexual orientation and gender identity in 11 E&E countries (COWI & DIHR, 2010a; COWI & DIHR, 2010b; COWI & DIHR, 2010c; COWI & DIHR, 2010d; COWI & DIHR, 2010e; COWI & DIHR, 2010f; COWI & DIHR, 2010g; COWI & DIHR, 2010h; COWI & DIHR, 2010i; COWI & DIHR, 2010j; COWI & DIHR, 2010k).

16. Pride parades have not been attempted in Albania, Armenia, Azerbaijan, Bosnia and Herzegovina, Georgia, and Kosovo. A parade was cancelled in Montenegro in 2011 (U.S. State Department, 2012). Events in Republic of Macedonia and Georgia that were held in 2012 have been characterized as a gay Pride marches. (Stojneto, 2012; BBC News, 2012; Euronews, 2013). Skopje Pride appears to be planned for the summer of 2013 (LGBT United Macedonia, 2013).

17. Some feel that LGBT Pride marches are inappropriate methods for achieving social integration and may actually mobilize violence against LGBT people. This particularly applies to transgender people who are often more physically visible than LGB people. Therefore, branding the parades using "LGBT" may be perceived as inaccurate and reflective of a "LGB agenda" that in actuality excludes transgender issues (K. Sabir, personal communication, 19 March 2012).

Gathering spaces. Both state officials (including law enforcement) and private individuals have targeted private places such as LGBT centers and offices where LGBT people gather, and clubs and bars. Attacks include graffiti and intimidation; serious property destruction; and physical assaults on staff and people in the space or leaving it, including both youth and adults (Russian LGBT Network, 2011; COWI & DIHR, 2010c; G&D, ILGA Europe, & Global Rights, 2009; GSA, 2011; Human Rights Watch, 2013). An example that received much attention online was the severe damage done to the LGBT-friendly bar DIY in Armenia in May 2012 —first by a homemade bomb attack and then property destruction that included graffiti identifying "LGBT people as targets" (Krikorian, 2012; Human Rights Watch, 2013). Government officials such as the Deputy Speaker of Parliament spoke out in support of the attack, and bail of approximately US$2,500 was paid by two members of parliament from the ARF party (Armenian Weekly, 2012).

Laws on "homosexual propaganda." The desire in some countries to silence the LGBT population's free expression and limit their capability to organize to defend their rights is starkly apparent in recently enacted and proposed legislation banning "homosexual propaganda." This legislation limits public discussion and displays of materials (e.g., posters and flags) that are supportive of LGBT people. The concept of criminalizing "homosexual propaganda to minors" was first applied in the Russian province of Ryazan in 2006. By July 2013, such national legislation[18] was in place in Russia in addition to that already in place in nine oblasts and St. Petersburg (Human Rights Watch, 2013).[19] Many stories of arrest and suppression are receiving worldwide attention in light of the upcoming Olympic Games, which will be held in Sochi, Russia in February 2014 (The Guardian 2013; Lally, 2013). Legislators have passed similar laws in several Moldovan cities, with one being overturned as unconstitutional by a local court of appeals (RFE/RL's Moldovan Service, 2013).

Countries in the E&E region that intend to enter the European Union tend to temper their official government stances; government officials more often voice individual opinions rather than promoting national legislation. In Ukraine, for example, the draft legislation on "homosexual propaganda," which passed its first reading, has stalled and there are reports that the labor code will be amended to prohibit discrimination based on sexual orientation in order to speed the European Union's process of visa liberalization (Bielecki, 2013).[20] In Moldova, an anti-homosexual propaganda amendment to the national Code of Administrative Offenses was overturned in October 2013 by lawmakers in the run up to Eastern Partnership Summit in Vilnius in November 2013 (Radio Free Europe/Radio Liberty, 2013a).

Right to Privacy. Exercising the right to keep one's sexual orientation or gender identity away from public scrutiny is challenging. All reports on the situation of LGBT people from across the region note that LGBT people are afraid to report crimes to police because they fear exposing their sexual orientation or gender identity to friends, family, and employers. Anecdotal accounts indicate that such worries are well founded. In multiple countries, LGBT people who have contact with the police have been forced to give information on their personal contacts who are also LGBT, and police have sought out others perceived to be homosexual (Nash Mir, 2013 & 2007; Radoman et al., 2011; MASSO, Global Rights, &ILGA-Europe, 2008). In addition, some LGBT people reported the invasion of their privacy by colleagues and classmates who revealed their sexual orientation or gender identity.

Freedom from cruel, inhumane or degrading treatment and punishment. LGBT people are subjected to violent abuse from their families, police, strangers, and organized LGBT opposition groups. Reports provide a picture of the range of mistreatment that occurs: arrest and beating of transgender persons and gay men while in custody in Azerbaijan; violent incidents against LGBT people in Serbia involving slurs, spitting, kicks, punches, and knife attacks in public places; physical attacks on Pride parade organizers by demonstrators in Ukraine; and in the Republic of Macedonia, incidences of rape of gay men were reported. Cases of physical, sexual, and psychological violence and abuse as well as LBT women's forced marriage and rape were recorded in a 2012 Convention on the

---

18. The federal law in Russia was changed to not use the term homosexual. Instead, it outlaws the "Promotion of non-traditional sexual relations among minors" (Russian Gazette, 2013). Regional laws do specify homosexual.

19. Some observers anticipated that the Russian laws would increase the number of LGBT refugees (Radio Free Europe, 2012). There are examples of those with financial means seeking refugee status (Gessen, 2013; CBC News, 2013).

20. For more information on the draft law, see Stern, 2012.

Elimination of Discrimination Against Women (CEDAW) submission for Georgia and in reports from Azerbaijan and Serbia (G&D, ILGA Europe & Global Rights, 2009; Natsvlishvili & Aghdgomelashvili, 2012).

SOCIO-ECONOMIC HUMAN RIGHTS VIOLATIONS

Prevailing legal codes regarding non-discrimination that may provide a means for recourse over the long term generally make little difference in the daily, local lives of LGBT individuals—in how they experience interaction with those who provide, withhold, or affect the delivery of vital services or sources of income. Across the E&E region, country reports and testimonies show that hiding one's sexual orientation when accessing health, housing, and education services is common and is considered necessary for employment (see Appendix 4b for examples).

Education. Education systems perpetuate negative stereotypes through curricula known to negatively characterize LGBT people and create obstacles that hamper LGBT students' learning by not addressing hostility they face from students and staff. No official policies appear to be in place regarding SOGI that would guide the actions of teachers and administrators (cf. Stakic, 2011). The documents reviewed for this report indicate that they tend to react in a variety of mostly negative ways.

Curricula. The International Planned Parenthood Federation European Network (2011) indicates that most schools in the E&E region do not teach general content on human sexuality. Textbooks and curricula on life skills and relationships appear to either exclude references to diverse sexuality and gender expressions, or present the subject in negative terms (COWI & DIHR, 2010g; COWI & DIHR, 2010j; COWI & DIHR, 2010k). In Bosnia and Herzegovina, for example, textbooks were reported to define homosexuality as a "disease or deviation" (COWI & DIHR, 2010d). A few lobbying efforts have been successful in getting such content removed. In 2012, offensive content was removed from medical textbooks in Albania in 2012 and from Macedonian secondary school textbooks (Pink Embassy, 2012; U.S. Department of State, 2012; ILGA-Europe, 2013a).[21] Local youth and adult NGO trainers provide free sexual education training in the context of healthy lifestyles training, but their reach is relatively limited, and their goals trend towards decreasing the prevalence of disease and unhealthy habits rather than building tolerance (e.g., Y-PEER; Association for Health Education and Research Macedonia). A few projects have been implemented with a goal of increasing tolerance, but they are not widespread.[22]

School environment. Schools and colleges are not safe places for LGBT people to openly reveal their sexual orientation because of bullying, violence, harassment, and mockery by teachers, professors, and other students (COWI & DIHR, 2010g; COWI & DIHR, 2010h; Durkovic, 2008; GSA, 2012; Nash Mir, 2013).[23] LGBT students report that this hostile environment interferes with learning and retention of knowledge. The explicit nature of verbally harassing threats, homophobic slurs, and sexual remarks leaves no doubt as to the reason LGBT students are targeted for such treatment. There have been a few instances of institutional discrimination in the region in the form of dismissal from teaching or expulsion from school, but more research is needed to determine its extent (COWI & DIHR, 2010g; GSA, 2011; Kochetkov & Kirichenko, 2008; GenderDoc-M, Global Rights, ILGA-Europe and the International Human Rights Clinic, & Harvard Law School, 2009).

Employment. Data from across the region confirm that LGBT people tend to keep their sexual orientation and gender identity hidden (if possible) in the workplace to avoid discrimination in the hiring process, harassment or bullying at work, or dismissal (Durkovic, 2008; COWI & DIHR, 2010a-k; U.S. Department of State, 2011; 2012). In instances where their identities becomes known—willingly or unwillingly—LGBT people have reported such discrimination occurs because of their SOGI, while employers attribute it to other reasons (cf. U.S. Department of State 2010; U.S. Department of State, 2011; Zinchenkov, et al., 2011; COWI & DIHR, 2010[24]). Seeking redress for

---

21. In Moldova negative references to homosexuality as a disease or deviation were removed from medical school curricula, but some educators did not heed the change and continued to relay such information (GenderDoc-M, 2011c).

22. For example, in 2009, a youth group from the NGO Human Rights House in Bosnia and Herzegovina visited students in schools in order to present information to the effect that homosexuality is not a disease or a crime, as well as on sex and gender. They were able to visit nine out of 25 targeted schools—even though the Ministry of Education did not give permission, some school directors did cooperate (COWI & DIHR, 2010d). Earlier, in 2007, UNICEF attempted to launch a life skills program that included information on sexual behavior, tolerance, and homosexuality—it was removed from schools due to broad-based religious opposition (COWI & DIHR, 2010g).

23. In some instances, administrators have denied admittance to LGBT students (Ivantchenko, 2010).

24. Additional sources include COWI & DIHR, 2010a; COWI & DIHR, 2010b; COWI & DIHR, 2010c; COWI & DIHR, 2010d; COWI & DIHR, 2010e; COWI & DIHR, 2010f; COWI & DIHR, 2010g; COWI & DIHR, 2010h; COWI & DIHR, 2010i; COWI & DIHR, 2010j; COWI & DIHR, 2010k.

employment discrimination based on SOGI is challenging. There are numerous anecdotal descriptions of the difficulty facing LGBT people making this claim. In Belarus, for example, it was reported that the editor of a gay website was fired from the British American Tobacco company (Canning, 2011). While the company stated that his employment was ended because of performance issues, the editor disagreed because other employees had told him it was because the head of his department learned that he was gay. He said that he had not received any negative feedback on his performance.

Because of their often heightened visibility, transgender peoples' stories regarding the workplace indicate that they cannot obtain employment or eventually leave their jobs because of harassment and bullying if they are employed at the time they begin the physical transition (COWI & DIHR, 2010c; Ghilascu, 2011; Ivantchenko, 2010). A Moldovan high school teacher, for example, was forced to quit her job in 2008 when she began hormone treatment for gender transition (GenderDoc-M et al, 2009). As a result of difficulty encountered when trying to change names and gender markers on documents, transgender people have sometimes not been able to claim their employment experience prior to changing their gender identity (COWI & DIHR, 201e; COWI & DIHR, 2010k; Ivantchenko, 2010).

Because it is so difficult for transgender people to maintain or obtain employment, they accept jobs without secure contracts or benefits and there are many cases of transgender women ending up in sex work (Kirichenko, 2011; COWI & DIHR, 2010a; COWI & DIHR, 2010c; COWI & DIHR, 2010g; G&D, 2009). Although providing a source of income, the sex work industry leaves transgender individuals vulnerable to violence from police and clients and at greater risk for HIV and other health care concerns.

THE STORY OF V.L., SERBIA.

The first time I was insulted was at the beginning of September 2010 when I came out as a gay man. I had the most problems with the Assistant Manager of the firm where I work. Once at a coffee break, he said to other workers right in front of me that no one should drink coffee from my cup, because who knows to whom I gave oral sex right before. At the beginning of October 2010 he said that "I was ill because faggots f***ed my brains out," after which one of the employees joined in and told others "not to turn their backs on me, so that I wouldn't rape and infect someone."

At the beginning of November 2010, I took sick leave, in order to get away at least a little bit from that pressure, since I didn't get any support or understanding from the General Manager after I complained to him about all those insults. He told me to sue them privately, because it was none of his business. That same manager told me a day or two after the 2010 gay parade that he wasn't able to take his wife out to lunch because of us fags.

I returned to work at the beginning of February 2011 and the verbal torture continued. The Assistant Manager told me he was disgusted by me, and one of the employees added that "he felt as if he passed by a carcass" when he would pass by me. That employee always keeps calling me a faggot, keeps saying that he will smack me at the first chance and threatening that I will never again be able to go into my village if I complain to you about all this. Recently, a couple of days ago, he told me the best thing for me would be an axe or a bat to the head, and then under the ground! This morning when I came to work, one of the employees asked me whether I could sit down on the chair and whether they f***ed me out real good last night. I can no longer stand this, and I'm afraid they will just fire me so that they don't have to look at me any more. I don't know what to do.

A few weeks after V.L. spoke to GSA, his employment was terminated. The Legal Service of GSA began a labor dispute to annul that decision and the proceedings are still in progress.

Excerpt from GSA, 2012

Note: Serbia's Gay Straight Alliance has annually documented such stories since 2007. LGBT NGOs in other E&E countries (e.g., Nash Mir in Ukraine, Gender Doc-M in Moldova, and Organization Q in Bosnia and Herzegovina) also document individuals' stories of employment discrimination and issues reports.

Health care. Health care professionals lack training and skills in delivering care to LGBT people and often exhibit discriminatory attitudes. The belief within the medical profession that homosexuality is an illness is real (Durkovic, 2008; COWI & DIHR, 2010g; COWI & DIHR, 2010i; Nash Mir, 2013; Natsvlishvili & Aghdgomelashvili, 2012).

Access to and delivery of health services to transgender people are serious problems across the region (Ivantchenko, 2010, Kirichenko, 2011). There is anecdotal evidence of medical professionals refusing to treat transgender women (COWI & DIHR, 2010a; COWI & DIHR, 2010c). In Albania, for example, treatment of an injured transgender woman was delayed for 45 minutes by a guard denying entry to a hospital and a doctor allegedly saying "one pederast less, let him die" (ILGA-Europe, 2011d).

In countries where sexual reassignment is legally recognized (Belarus, Bosnia and Herzegovina, Georgia, Montenegro, Russia, and Ukraine), legal recognition is only extended to those who have been given the diagnosis of Gender Identity Disorder (GID). [25] Table 4 presents legal requirements relevant to transgender people in the E&E region.

In the region, psychological, medical, and legal processes of changing sex take several years, and those going through them often confront obstacles, including the time, cost[26], and effort (including travel) as well as medical personnel trying to dissuade a person from undergoing surgery, and the procurement of new identification and other documents (Ivantchenko, 2011; Russian LGBT Network, 2011). Transgender people undergoing the hormone replacement therapy used to reassign gender (and "treat" Gender Dysphoria, which is still referred to as Gender Identity Disorder in the region) must also deal with its effects. Also, access to gender reassignment requires sterilization (Gayten-LGBT, Transgender Europe & ILGA Europe, 2013).The process can be very destabilizing emotionally (K. Sabir, personal communication, 19 March 2012).

Reports indicate that medical gender reassignment is not easily accessible in the region. In most countries, the process, whether officially prescribed or not, is complex and bureaucratic (COWI & DIHR, 2010e; COWI & DIHR, 2010g). In some countries, such as Ukraine, Serbia, and Russia, a person may find specialists who can see them through the entire gender reassignment process, including surgery; in other countries, such as Albania, Azerbaijan, Armenia, and Republic of Macedonia, service is piecemeal or nonexistent (Barlovac, 2010; COWI & DIHR, 2010a; COWI & DIHR 2010b; COWI & DIHR, 2010c; COWI & DIHR, 2010f).[27] This situation means that many people who wish to undergo gender reassignment must leave their countries of origin. Montenegro and Serbia are the only E&E countries which cover gender reassignment surgery under a national healthcare system (Zapata, 2012; Astraea Lesbian Foundation for Justice, 2012). Availability, however, still does not guarantee easy access.

In Ukraine, because the Ministry of Health commission that approves medical sex reassignment does not meet according to a schedule, some people have had to wait for up to a decade. This has physical health implications if they have been or are continuing to take hormone or other treatments for a long time and mental health implications for patients who are in a transitional "limbo," unable to live completely in their true gender and integrate into society (Ivantchenko, 2012, Kirichenko, 2011). However, this does not occur only in Ukraine. Throughout the region, many transgender people access medication, such as hormone treatments, through the Internet and other informal means, bypassing their countries' medical establishment. This self-medication can be very dangerous to their health and wellbeing due to lack of control of the quality of the drugs, incorrect apportioning of doses, and fear of seeking treatment for side effects (COWI & DIHR, 2010g).

---

25. As of 2013, GID is referred to as gender dysphoria and not considered a disorder by the *Diagnostic and Statistical Manual of Mental Disorders* of the American Psychiatric Association (Lowder, 2012).

26. Serbia has been noted as a country with affordable and available facilities for sex-reassignment surgery and is becoming a destination for those from the E&E region as well as Western Europe. For Serbs, the costs are subsidized by national health insurance (Bilefsky, 2012). Russia, Turkey, and Thailand have also been noted as destinations (COWI & DIHR, 2010c). A change to Montenegrin law in 2012 ensures that 80 percent of the costs of the entire medical gender-reassignment process (psychotherapy, hormone therapy, and surgery) are covered by state-funded healthcare (Zapata, 2012).

27. According to the 2013 Rainbow Index from ILGA-Europe, it is possible to access gender reassignment procedures in Belarus, Georgia, Montenegro, Russia, and Ukraine (ILGA-Europe, 2013a). It is not clear why Serbia is not included since multiple sources indicate that procedures are available (Bilefsky, D., 2012; Barlovac, 2010).

HIV/AIDS. In the E&E region, MSM and transgender women are key vulnerable groups who are targeted by HIV/AIDS prevention work. "Unfortunately there [are] no comprehensive data to fully identify the role of this population in the HIV epidemic, and studies by major international AIDS organizations estimate that official studies in these countries underestimate the infected population" (AIDSTAR 2, 2010). They are regarded by USAID, UNAIDS, the World Health Organization (WHO), and the Global Fund to Fight AIDS, Tuberculosis and Malaria (GFATM) as one of the most at-risk populations (MARPs) for HIV and AIDS. Transgender women are often grouped with MSM for HIV service programs. This is problematic in that transgender women do not identify as men, and their HIV prevention, treatment, and care needs are substantially different. High-risk sexual behaviors prevalent among these groups in the region include multiple sexual partners and failure to use condoms during intercourse. In some countries, anecdotally high use of injection drugs by MSM and transgender women compounds their risk. Programs for MSM and transgender women are stymied by a lack of political will and their small scale. Because of the stigmatization of MSM, transgender women, and other LGBT people, prevention and care programs are underfunded and not comprehensive—they focus only on delivering prevention services and not on the other parts of a comprehensive approach to address HIV and sexual health. Among younger MSM, a general lack of awareness of HIV/AIDS transmission routes has been noted across the E&E region (AIDSTAR 2, 2010; COWI & DIHR, 2010b)

Housing. There is little data on discrimination against LGBT people in housing. Much available information focuses on young people sharing an apartment and on youth that are kicked out of the family home. For a variety of reasons, it is common for young people in the E&E region to live in the family home until they are married (COWI & DIHR, 2010g). Students and employed young LGBT people do rent apartments in order to live alone or with a partner (Carroll & Quinn, 2009). They need to present themselves as friends rather than partners to prospective landlords (COWI & DIHR, 2010a; COWI & DIHR, 2010j). Landlord discrimination against LGBT people can be virtually impossible to prove. If neighbors become aware of a same-sex relationship, the couple's tenancy could be vulnerable. In Russia, for example, there have been reports of community members harassing and intimidating neighbors they believe are gay men (Kochetkov & Kirichenko, 2008).

Access to family-based social benefits and responsibilities. Same-sex partners are not recognized as domestic partners and same-sex couples or families in any of the E&E countries. They are disadvantaged in terms of health care decisions, pension schemes, social benefits, taxes, insurance, and other areas where family status is relevant for opposite-sex couples. In addition, though with limited evidence, it appears that lesbians can have trouble inheriting or receiving compensation for their share of a family land, despite laws mandating familial inheritance rights. An individual in Georgia, for example, had to take the case to court (Natsvlishvili & Aghdgomelashvili, 2012).

IV. STATUS OF VEHICLES FOR THE PROTECTION OF LGBT PEOPLE'S BASIC HUMAN RIGHTS IN THE E&E REGION

A. INTERNATIONAL LAWS AND MECHANISMS

THE UNITED NATIONS

The right to equality and non-discrimination is recognized in Article 2 of the Universal Declaration of Human Rights and is elaborated in UN human rights conventions.[28] All E&E countries except for Kosovo[29] have ratified six legally binding covenants and conventions:

- International Covenant on Civil and Political Rights (ICCPR)
- International Covenant on Economic, Social and Cultural Rights (ICESCR)
- Convention against Torture and Other Cruel, Inhuman or Degrading Treatment or Punishment (CAT)
- Convention on the Rights of the Child (CRC)
- Convention on the Elimination of All Forms of Discrimination against Women (CEDAW)
- International Convention on the Elimination of All Forms of Racial Discrimination (ICERD)
- Convention relating to the Status of Refugees (CRSR)

Either in case law or in General Comments, the treaty bodies overseeing the ICCPR and the ICESCR have set precedents by including SOGI as grounds of discrimination.[30] This allows for parallel interpretation in subsequent treaties.

Signatory country governments are required to report on the implementation of these conventions and NGOs are invited to submit "shadow" reports with additional, and sometimes contradictory, information. The UN Human Rights Council's Universal Periodic Review (UPR) process, initiated in 2008, also offers a similar opportunity. In addition, UN Special Rapporteurs, both thematic and geographic, and the UN Office of the High Commissioner for Human Rights issues reports that include human rights violations suffered by LGBT people at the hands of both government and private actors (OHCHR, 2012).

Albania, Armenia, Bosnia and Herzegovina, Georgia, Republic of Macedonia, Montenegro, Serbia, and Ukraine signed this UN Human Rights Council Joint Statement on Sexual Orientation and Gender Identity in March, 2011. It called for a study of discriminatory laws and practices and convening a panel discussion (United Nations General Assembly, 2011). The panel discussion was held in March 2012.[31]

EUROPEAN INSTITUTIONS

Three European institutions are particularly relevant to ensuring and securing the protection of human rights, including those of LGBT people: the Council of Europe (CoE), the European Union (EU), and the Organization for Security and Co-operation in Europe (OSCE). Their mandates are very broad and each addresses numerous issues that affect peace, security, social wellbeing, and economic growth.

---

28. The Un Declaration of Human Rights, while not a convention with signatories, is considered to be a part of customary international law (OHCHR, 2009).

29. Kosovo, although not a UN member state, under UN Security Council Resolution 1244, is obliged by international law to respect the ICCPR as a successor to Yugoslavia. It recognized that obligation in its own legal order through its acceptance of the Ahtisaari Plan and by article 22(1) of its 2008 constitution.

30. UN Human Rights Committee, Toonen v. Australia, Communication No. 488/1992 30, March 1994, CCPR/ C/50/D/488/1992, paragraph 8.7; UN Human Rights Committee, Young v. Australia, Communication No. 941/2000, 6 August 2003, CCPR/C/78/D/941/2000; UN Human Rights Committee, X v. Colombia, Communication No. 1361/2005, 14 May 2007, CCPR/C/89/D/1361/2005. The UN Committee on Economic, Social and Cultural Rights, General Comment No. 20 on Non-Discrimination in relation to Economic, Social and Cultural Rights, 2009, paragraph 32 says "States Parties should ensure that a person's sexual orientation is not a barrier to realizing Covenant rights, for example, in accessing survivor's pension rights. In addition, gender identity is recognized as among the prohibited grounds of discrimination; for example, persons who are transgender, transsexual or intersex often face serious human rights violations, such as harassment in schools or in the workplace."

31. For the content of this discussion, see http://arc-international.net/global-advocacy/human-rights-council/hrc19/panel-summary

Council of Europe (CoE). Forty-seven countries are members of the CoE (CoE, n.d.b), which promotes cooperation among European countries with the following objectives:

- Protect human rights, pluralist democracy and the rule of law

- Promote awareness and encourage the development of Europe's cultural identity and diversity

- Find common solutions to the challenges facing European society

- Consolidate democratic stability in Europe by backing political, legislative and constitutional reform (CoE, n.d.c)

Most countries in the E&E region are party to the CoE's European Convention on Human Rights (ECHR) by virtue of their membership in the CoE, all members of which must ratify the ECHR at their earliest opportunity (Parliamentary Assembly, CoE Parliamentary Assembly, 1994). Only Kosovo and Belarus are not members (CoE, n.d.a), although Kosovo is expected to be the 48th signatory to the ECHR and has generally aligned its national legislation with its principles.

The Convention established the European Court of Human Rights (ECtHR) [32], which is an international court that "rules on individual or State applications alleging violations of the civil and political rights set out in the European Convention on Human Rights" (ECtHR, 2012). When it is alleged that government officials or civil servants are complicit in human rights violations, victims may turn to the ECtHR and build a case based on the breach of different articles, such as those dealing with torture, liberty and security, privacy, expression, association and effective remedy, and discrimination (cf. ECtHR Case-Law; ILGA-Europe, 2011c).[33] The ECtHR has already applied Article 14 of the Convention(the ban on discrimination) to cases of discrimination based on sexual orientation and gender identity and issued judgments in favor of the plaintiffs (CoE, 2000).[34]

In addition to the Convention and ECtHR, the CoE developed the world's first international treaty to explicitly include both sexual orientation and gender identity in its clause on non-discrimination and put it forward for signature in 2011 (CoE, 2011c).[35]

CoE also provides guidance and technical assistance to its member countries concerning the conduct of state institutions and bodies in relation to LGBT discrimination and enacted the first intergovernmental agreement to address discrimination on grounds of sexual orientation and gender identity (CoE, 2010a).[36] It is a document of great importance to LGBT advocates and their allies in the region as it provides clear guidance on state obligations. The CoE helps countries implement this guidance through police training, sharing knowledge, and helping draft national action plans (CoE, n.d.b). It is too early to assess the impact of this guidance in the region, but LGBT NGOs in the Republic of Macedonia, Montenegro,

As with the decisions of most international treaty bodies, the effectiveness of ECHR rulings can be compromised by a state's unwillingness to comply. The banning of Moscow Pride marches in 2006, 2007, and 2008 was taken up by ECHR in the case Alexysev v. Russia. Though the court found that the ban constituted violations to freedom of assembly (Article 11), the right to effective legal remedy (Article 13) and Article 14, Pride marches continue to be banned in Moscow (ECtHR, 2011; RIA Novosti, 2013).

---

32. Not to be confused with the Court of Justice of the European Union or the International Court of Justice. The European Court of Human Rights rules on alleged violations of the European Convention on Human Rights for the CoE (European Court of Human Rights, 2012).

33. Case law shows that Article 14 and Protocol No. 12 of the ECHR include grounds for claims of discrimination that are not explicitly named in the original Convention, including SOGI. However, Kosovo has not signed or ratified Protocol No. 12 of the ECHR; Azerbaijan, Moldova, and Russia have signed, but not ratified, this protocol. The protocol may be accessed here: http://conventions.coe.int/Treaty/Commun/QueVoulezVous.asp?NT=177&CM=7&DF=01/08/2013&CL=ENG

34. See the ECtHR factsheets on sexual orientation and gender identity issues for examples of relevant cases and decisions (ECtHR, 2013a; ECtHR, 2013b).

35. Annex E of the CoE's European Social Charter (ESC) includes an open-ended non-discrimination clause, although SOGI is not directly mentioned. In addition to national reports, governments are free to submit comments from NGOs for review by the committee overseeing the ESC. Georgia and Ukraine submitted comments that addressed SOGI-related discrimination in employment (Inclusive Foundation and ILGA-Europe, 2008 [*report unavailable*], ILGA-Europe, 2012e).

36. In March 2012, the CoE appointed Mr. Håkon Haugli as the first Parliamentary Assembly Council of Europe (PACE) General rapporteur on the rights of LGBT people (CoE, 2012a). This office opened a LGBT Issues Unit, and initiated a 28-month project in September 2011 with the goal of helping the governments of Montenegro, Serbia, and Albania create strong cross-sectoral LGBT policies (CoE, 2012b).

Albania, Serbia, Bosnia and Herzegovina, Georgia, and Ukraine attest to actively utilizing the related Toolkit (CoE, 2010b) or working with CoE offices in their countries (ILGA-Europe, 2010).

European Union (EU). Republic of Macedonia, Montenegro, and Serbia are currently candidate countries to join the EU; Albania, Bosnia and Herzegovina, and Kosovo are potential candidate countries (European Commission, 2013). All are expected to align their human rights laws and law enforcement with European standards in order to receive pre-accession assistance and join the EU. As a part of accession processes, the EU is becoming more demanding regarding the application of human rights law and standards to LGBT people. The European Commission is using accession reports to examine relevant legal frameworks, and policies as well as discrimination and aggression against LGBT people, assistance provided to LGBT people, and other government actions (The European Parliament's Intergroup on LGBT Rights, 2012).

There are agreements between the EU and E&E countries that are not candidates or potential candidates which seem to be platforms for engagement. The European Neighborhood and Partnership Instrument (ENPI), the European Instrument for Democracy and Human Rights (EIDHR), the Eastern Partnership (EaP), and the Partnership and Cooperation Agreements (PCAs) provide frameworks for political dialogue that enables convergence of "their positions on international issues of mutual concern, stability, security and respect for democracy and human rights" (European Union, 2010).[37] These partnerships involve financial and technical support in order to improve respect for human rights, strengthen civil society, promote democratic reform, and support international cooperation on the protection of human rights (European Commission, n.d.).

Reports and news articles from E&E countries indicate that a predilection toward EU membership is more influential than institutions such as the CoE on countries' choices to protect the rights of LGBT people (Bielecki, 2013; Roudik, 2012; Sequi, 2013). For example, the upcoming Eastern Partnership meeting appears to have spurred Moldova and Ukraine into action (Radio Free Europe/Radio Liberty, 2013a; Globa, 2013).

Organization for Security and Co-operation in Europe (OSCE). The OSCE's Office for Democratic Institutions and Human Rights (ODIHR) helps OSCE members implement their commitments on human rights, tolerance, and non-discrimination. It provides assistance to governments (e.g., legislators, police, and judiciary) through knowledge-sharing and consensus-building activities that build their capacity to protect human rights and human rights defenders. OSCE Missions also train NGOs on topics such as identifying and reporting hate crimes, which include crimes against LGBT people (OSCE, n.d.c). OSCE created the Tolerance and Non-Discrimination Information System (TANDIS), a database used for collecting and tracking laws, policies, tools, guides, and high-level meeting reports on tolerance and discrimination (OSCE, n.d.a). Homophobia is one of the key issues tracked by the database (OSCE/ODIHR, n.d.a).

B. NATIONAL LEVEL LAWS AND MECHANISMS

Across the region, there is little evidence of the political will to adopt and enforce legislative and policy measures that combat crime and discrimination against LGBT persons. There is also little effort to ensure that victims can obtain justice. Where there are laws on non-discrimination, implementation and enforcement appear to be deficient. Limited knowledge and understanding among law enforcement officers about the rights of LGBT people tends to affect their work.

LAWS

Same-sex sexual activity is legal in criminal law across the region as it was decriminalized by most countries in the 1990s and in the Caucasus in the early 2000s. In comparison, decriminalization occurred in Poland in 1932, Slovenia and Croatia in 1977, and Romania in 1996 (Waaldijk, 2009).

Currently across the region, there are very few national-level legal or policy mechanisms that include protection from discrimination based on SOGI. Albania and Montenegro are the only E&E countries that have comprehensive non-discrimination laws that include sexual orientation and gender identity (applicable in areas such as education, health protection, social insurance, and employment). Table 3 below lists current legal prohibitions against discrimination based on SOGI in the E&E region.

---

37. See http://ec.europa.eu/world/enp/pdf/oj_l310_en.pdf, http://ec.europa.eu/europeaid/where/worldwide/eidhr/index_en.htm, and http://www.easternpartnership.org/content/eap-at-a-glance for more information

TABLE 3. LEGALLY RECOGNIZED AREAS WITH PROTECTION AGAINST LGBT DISCRIMINATION IN THE E&E REGION

Country and Existing Legislation	Protected Status	Areas Covered
Albania Law on Protection from Discrimination	SOGI	Ed, EE, G&S, He, Ho, PP
Armenia (n/a)	n/a	
Azerbaijan (n/a)	n/a	
Belarus (n/a)	n/a	
Bosnia and Herzegovina Law on Prohibition of Discrimination	SO	Ed, EE, G&S, He, Ho, SP
Georgia Labour Code of Georgia (Law No. 4113 of 17 December 2010)	SO	EE
Kosovo The Anti-discrimination Law	SO	Ed, EE, G&S, He, Ho, PP, SP
Republic of Macedonia Labor Law	*	
Moldova Law on Equal Opportunities	SO	Ed, EE, G&S, He, Ho, SP
Montenegro Law on Prevention and Protection against Discrimination	SOGI	Ed, EE
Russia (n/a)	n/a	
Serbia Law on the Prohibition of Discrimination Law on Youth	 SO SOGI	Ed, EE
Ukraine (n/a)**	n/a	

Sources: Assembly of the Republic of Albania, 2010; Parliamentary Assembly of Bosnia and Herzegovina- House of Representatives, 2009; Georgian Trade Unions Confederation, 2010; Assembly of Kosovo, 2001; ILO, 2012; Roudik, 2012; Orrick, OSCE/ODIHR, n.d.b; Herrington & Sutcliffe LLP, 2009; EC & COE, n.d.).

Notes: Ed = education, EE = employment and entrepreneurship, G&S = goods and services, He = healthcare, Ho = housing, PP = political participation, SP = social protection

* Although the draft Law on Preventing and Protection Against Discrimination in the Republic of Macedonia included sexual orientation as a protected characteristic, the law passed by the Macedonian government in 2010 did not (Coalition of Sexual and Health Rights of Marginalized Communities, 2011). While labor law in Republic of Macedonia appears to prohibit discrimination against applicants or employees on the basis of sexual orientation, it is not clear which law has overriding authority.

**Draft Law on Amendments to Certain Legislative Acts of Ukraine on Prevention and Combating Discrimination in Ukraine was stalled in committee as of May, 2013 (Verhovna Rada of Ukraine, 2013). The bill adds sexual orientation after sex in Article 21 of the Labor Code. Owing to large protests, discussion of the law has been tabled (Radio Free Europe/Radio Liberty, 2013b).

Where constitutional equality provisions exist—Azerbaijan, Georgia, Republic of Macedonia, and Montenegro— they appear to allow scope for SOGI to be included, although there are no examples of case law where this has been tested. It appears that for SOGI to be included as a status, it needs to be specified in laws and legal codes or clarified in case law. For example, although the *Constitution of Montenegro* prohibits inflicting or encouraging hatred or intolerance on any grounds, the Criminal Code of Montenegro mentions only national, racial, and religious hatred and intolerance (CoE, n.d.).[38]

Other than in non-discrimination legislation, the prohibition of SOGI-based discrimination is codified in only a handful of laws in the region. In Moldova, sexual orientation is mentioned in the Law on Application of Lie Detector, the Polygraph Law on Asylum, and the Law on Freedom of Expression. In Serbia, the Criminal Code has been amended to include steeper penalties for crimes committed out of hatred for statuses including SOGI (Republic of Serbia, 2012). Laws on labor, higher education, public information, and broadcasting also reference sexual orientation.

---

38. Overviews of the legal situation in each country may be found in the COWI & DIHR, 2010a-k reports. They are listed individually in the reference list, but may be accessed as a group at http://www.coe.int/t/commissioner/activities/themes/lgbt/nationalreports_en.asp

Hate crimes. [39] There are many examples of crimes that would likely be considered hate crimes or hate speech in the courts if countries had laws on bias-motivated crimes on the books and such laws were applied to SOGI-related crimes. [40] Albania and Georgia include SOGI as aggravating factors in offenses such as assault. Georgia amended its criminal code in March 2012 (Government of Georgia, 2012) to include SOGI-related bias as an aggravating circumstance that could increase the penalty in any crime, and Albania did so in May 2013. In addition, a new crime was added to the Albanian criminal code, the "distribution of racist, homophobic or xenophobic materials through systems of communication and information technology" (Historia IME, 2013a).

National HIV/AIDS strategies. To varying degrees, E&E countries include LGBT people in their HIV/AIDS prevention and treatment efforts. Prevention strategies are broadly aligned with the Joint UNAIDS HIV/AIDS Strategy, the Global Health Sector Strategy for HIV/AIDS, and the European Commission Communication on Combating HIV/AIDS in the EU, and are overseen by Ministries of Health or government-appointed National AIDS Committees. Interventions carried out according to these strategies include LGBT people by targeting populations they describe as MSM and WSW. All programs operate under Country Coordinating Mechanisms overseen by Ministries of Health in partnership with, and with funding from, UNAIDS and the Global Fund to Fight AIDS, Tuberculosis and Malaria (GFATM). Of the E&E countries, only Azerbaijan's national HIV/AIDS plan does not specify MSM as a vulnerable group to target (AIDSTAR 2, 2010).

Legal family and relationship recognition, social security/insurance. There are no legal provisions recognizing same-sex partners as family members in any E&E country. Thus, in terms of health, social benefits, taxes, insurance, and other areas where family status is important, LGBT people are not recognized as kin or next of kin and cannot access rights, responsibilities, and benefits equal to those of opposite-sex couples. [41] Albania, Armenia, Georgia, Republic of Macedonia, Moldova, Montenegro, Serbia, and Ukraine have updated or clarified existing laws through constitutional or legal reforms in order to specify that marriage legislation only applies to opposite sex couples. [42]

Regulations and laws affecting the official recognition of gender identity in relation to gender reassignment. Where legal recognition of gender reassignment exists in the E&E region, it is with the proviso of an initial diagnosis of gender dysphoria ("Gender Identity Disorder" is the term currently used in the region) and subsequent compulsory sterilization and divorce if married (in Bosnia and Herzegovina, only compulsory sterilization is required). In countries where there is no legal recognition of transgender people, the legal situation of transgender people who are married is very complicated and uncertain. Most countries require sex reassignment surgery to change a person's sex on official documents. In Ukraine, [43] Georgia, Moldova, and Serbia, for example, it is legal to change one's documents, but the unstandardized process may only be completed after surgery (U.S. Department of State, 2012; Ivantchenko, 2012; Jormarjidze, 2012; COWI & DIHR, 2010g; Gayten-LGBT, Transgender Europe, & ILGA Europe, 2013). [44] Russia alone does not require surgery, but the change is

---

39. A hate crime is a "criminal offense against a person or property motivated in whole or in part by an offender's bias against a race, religion, disability, ethnic origin or sexual orientation" (Federal Bureau of Investigation, n.d.) The Council of Europe defines the term hate speech so as to cover all forms of expression that spread, incite, promote or justify racial hatred, xenophobia, anti-Semitism or other forms of hatred based on intolerance, including: intolerance expressed by aggressive nationalism and ethnocentrism, discrimination and hostility against minorities, migrants and people of immigrant origin (Weber, 2009).

40. See the reference list for many resources that include stories of LGBT people who have experienced hate crimes and hate speech. In addition to the incidents noted in the section on types of human rights violations, examples of human rights violations included elsewhere in this report may also be examples of hate crimes or speech.

41. None of the reports cited in the reference list noted that same-sex partners were considered next of kin. Where mentioned, the reports noted that they are not recognized.

42. Constitutions may be found on Legislationline, a site managed by OSCE/ODIHR: http://legislationline.org/documents/section/constitutions.

43. In Ukraine, it is only possible to change the first name and surname arbitrarily before or after the sex marker on an ID document has been changed. The law only allows changing patronymics in cases of adoption or change of the father's name. A patronymic is part of the surname and is constructed using the father's first name and an ending based on a person's sex. It is common to hear patronymics used that follow Ukrainian and Russian language rules. All identity documents require patronymics in Ukraine and Russia. This is problematic especially for those who are undergoing hormone replacement therapy because the ending of a patronymic reveals a person's sex at birth, which might not match their current appearance, and patronyms are used widely in society to refer to individuals. (Ivantchenko, 2012).

44. Ivantchenko (2012) also notes that it is problematic that Ukraine's Sex Reassignment Commission does not meet regularly to approve sex reassignment surgery, and therefore "transgender persons who take hormones are forced live with the original documents that do not reflect their current status."

24

handwritten on current documents. Obtaining new documents requires an appeal to a court of law (COWI & DIHR, 2010i). An April 2013 report indicates that one person in Montenegro has received a new identity card without having undergone surgery, thus setting a new precedent (LGBT Forum Progress, 2013). However, multiple reports indicate that the methods used to change the gender marker or indicate that it has changed appear to be problematic because they do not ensure privacy (COWI & DIHR, 2010e; Ghilascu, 2011; Ivantchenko, 2010; Jomarijidze, 2012; Sindelar, 2013). In addition, in Russia, a social insurance number stays with a person for life. Because a record of an individual's sex accompanies the number, this document can expose a change in their gender identity (K. Sabir, personal communication, 19 March 2012).

Transgender people often carry documents that do not reflect their current gender. This can severely hamper a person's ability to live, work in the formal sector, travel, vote, study or verify their educational certifications, access health care, and engage in financial transactions.

TABLE 4. LEGAL REQUIREMENTS IMPORTANT TO TRANSGENDER PEOPLE IN THE E&E REGION

Country	Legally recognizes name change	Requires sterilization for gender reassignment	Requires divorce for gender reassignment	Allows change of sex on official documents to match gender identity
Albania		X	X	
Armenia		X	X	
Azerbaijan		X	X	X
Belarus	X	X	X	X
Bosnia and Herzegovina	X	X		
Georgia	X	X	X	X
Kosovo		X	X	
Republic of Macedonia	X	X	X	X
Moldova	X	X	X	X
Montenegro	X	X	X	X
Russia	X	X	X	X
Serbia	X	X	X	
Ukraine	X (Change to patronymic not permitted)	X	X	X

Sources: ILGA-Europe, 2013a, COWI & DIHR, 2010j

ILLUSTRATION: MOLDOVA

In Moldova, transgender people have significant difficulties changing the gender recorded in their identity documents because of a lack of legislation and guidance for local registration offices. Offices deal with each person on a case-by-case basis. Currently, transgender people are allowed to change their identity documents only after sexual reassignment surgery. As of the end of 2012, a pending court of appeals decision could give transgender people the right to change their gender on documents without completing gender reassignment surgery. Meanwhile, a non-binding recommendation was issued to lower courts to allow the gender recorded in civil documents to be changed before surgery. FtM transgender people have particular challenges when getting new documents because they need to get a military passport that is required for all males over 16. When, in rare cases, they are able to achieve this, the passport is stamped with a message that the individual is unfit for military service (COWI & DIHR, 2010g; Ghilascu, 2011; U.S. State Department, 2012).

Since 2012, the regional NGO ILGA-Europe has systematically analyzed countries' laws, statutes, and administrative practices in order to develop an index that rates countries based on their levels of protection of the human rights of LGBTI people. Countries are scored and ranked based on their laws and policies in the areas of respect for freedoms of assembly, association and expression; asylum; anti-discrimination; family recognition; protection against hate speech and hate crime; and legal gender recognition.[45] In 2013, the top three countries were the United Kingdom, Belgium, and Norway. The lowest ranked countries were Russia, Armenia, and Azerbaijan (ILGA-Europe, 2013b).

TABLE 5. ILGA-EUROPE'S RAINBOW INDEX, 2013

Country	Score	Rank	Country	Score	Rank
Albania	38	16	Republic of Macedonia	13	43
Armenia	8	48	Moldova	10	46
Azerbaijan	8	47	Montenegro	27	27
Belarus	14	41	Russia	7	49
Bosnia and Herzegovina	20	33	Serbia	25	28
Georgia	21	30	Ukraine	12	44
Kosovo	14	42			

Source: ILGA Europe, 2013b

IMPLEMENTATION OF LAWS AND MECHANISMS

There appears to be some implementation of laws and mechanisms. Given the recent adoption of non-discrimination laws that apply to SO and sometimes GI, it is difficult to accurately assess their implementation and enforcement. This section will look at the roles of national human rights institutions, the practices of law enforcement and the judiciary with regard to upholding rule of law across the board, and the effects of specific capacity-building efforts by regional organizations aiming to improve compliance with international laws and norms on the protection of LGBT people.

National human rights institutions (NHRIs). Since 2009, these institutions—known by various names and listed in Appendix 6—appear to be the primary state institutions in the E&E region charged with the protection of LGBT people's human rights in the context of violations by public authorities and in cases of inaction by public authorities when rights are violated by other parties (OHCHR, 2010). Annual reports and websites indicate that most appear to exclude the protection of LGBT people from their work. However, there have been positive developments in recent years:

- The 2011address by the Public Defender of Georgia, to a panel at the ILGA-Europe Annual Conference affirmed the human rights of LGBT people (WISG, 2011).

- Ombudsman offices in Serbia and Albania have been instrumental in drawing significant media and political attention to the human rights of LGBT people regarding freedom of assembly and expression.

- The 2013 report of the Ukrainian Parliamentary Commissioner for Human Rights recommended increasing accountability for bias-related crimes by including a list of attributes (including sexual orientation) as aggravating motives for crime (Ukrainian Parliament Commissioner for Human Rights, 2013).

Ombudspersons are limited to drawing attention to issues in national and international forums and acting as a government advisor. Their impact on protecting human rights related to SOGI is unclear. Some have partnerships with local LGBT NGOs. The Armenian Human Rights Defender, for example signed a memorandum of collaboration with PINK Armenia (PINK Armenia, 2011b).

Law enforcement and judicial systems. There is a pattern of negative interaction with police across the E&E region (Quinn, 2007; Radoman et al., 2011; U.S. Department of State, 2011). It is difficult to report discrimination or criminal attacks in E&E countries because most do not have laws specifically prohibiting discrimination based on

---

45. The methodology is not entirely clear, but countries are given points within categories regarding whether they are fully or partially compliant. The total percentage appears to be the number of points divided by the total possible score (ILGA-Europe, 2013c).

a person's SOGI, nor do they include SOGI as a basis for adjudicating hate crimes or speech (COWI & DIHR, 2010k; Parliamentary Assembly of Bosnia and Herzegovina, 2010). Officials responsible for enforcing the rule of law in the region appear to discriminate against LGBT people by not upholding the rule of law and carrying out justice as well as by further victimizing complainants and colluding with offenders (Durkovic, 2008; GenderDoc-M, 2011c; Zinchenkov, et al., 201U.S. Department of State 2010; U.S. Department of State 2011; U.S. Department of State 2012). When LGBT people are attacked and the police intervene in public, police have allegedly engaged in such actions as detaining victims of assault, sexually assaulting victims, mocking or harassing victims, threatening to out victims, and allowing attackers to leave the crime scene without following police procedures such as filing a report (COWI & DIHR, 2010c; COWI & DIHR, 2010h; GenderDoc-M, 2011c; Natsvlishvili & Aghdgomelashvili, 2012). (For more information on actual incidents, see Appendix 4a.) While the majority of interactions have not been positive, there is evidence of some arrests and prosecutions of those who commit crimes against LGBT people and increasing protection of LGBT people's rights to gather and express themselves[46] (Associated Press, 2013; COWI & DIHR, 2010a; COWI & DIHR, 2010b; GSA, 2012; Helsinki Committee for Human Rights of the Republic of Macedonia, 2011; Immigration and Refugee Board of Canada, 2011; BBC News, 2013; Savic, 2013).

Transgender people report especially severe and humiliating treatment by police. In particular, transgender women accused of sex work allege psychological, physical, and sexual violence when recounting their experiences with the police to local NGOs (COWI & DIHR, 2010a; COWI & DIHR, 2010b, COWI & DIHR, 2010g; COWI & DIHR, 2010f; COWI & DIHR, 2010g; Labrys, 2008).

There are indications that police sensitivity training for working with LGBT people is limited and that the contact information of trained police officers is not readily available (Radoman et al., 2011; Savic, 2013). Specific training for the purpose of protecting LGBT populations, however, is occurring under the auspices of the CoE. Such training may have played a role in the increasing level of protection of participants in Pride parades, such as the 2013 parade in Montenegro (Associated Press, 2013).

Examples of prosecutions and convictions for various crimes involving offenses such as threats, use of force, destruction of property, and verbal harassment against LGBT people are hard to come by in the E&E region. In the entire region, there appears to have been only one instance in which a leader of an organized group that committed an anti-LGBT hate crime was indicted and prosecuted.[47] Hate speech and death threats posted on the Internet are increasingly being recorded, but prosecution has only been mentioned in a few instances. In 2011, there was a judgment against an online news site for allowing hate speech during a chat (Boissevain, 2011), and a court in Serbia sentenced a person to a three-month jail term for threatening LGBT people via Facebook by creating a group called "500,000 Serbs against Gay Pride" (Human Rights Watch, 2013).

---

46. In Serbia, increased reporting and willingness to use legal institutions to obtain redress point toward positive change (GSA, 2012).

47. The leader of the Serbian extremist group Obraz, was sentenced to ten months in jail in March 2012 for inciting hatred and delivering death threats to LGBT people in the run-up to the 2009 Pride parade, which was never held because of security risks. In 2011, he was sentenced to two years in prison for inciting violence during the 2010 Pride, but the case was under appeal as of January 2013 (Human Rights Watch, 2013).

V. CAPACITY OF NGOS TO ADDRESS LGBT CONCERNS

A. LGBT NGOS AND ALLIES ACTIVE IN THE E&E REGION

LGBT and allied NGOs working to serve the LGBT community and advocate for change encounter barriers to their work related to their capacity and sustainability. There has not been a study of LGBT NGOs in the E&E region, but the CSO Sustainability Index, which has ranked regional CSOs in seven areas crucial to the strength and viability of CSOs, provides a useful framework for a general analysis. [48]

TABLE 6: SUSTAINABILITY REVIEW OF NATIONAL AND LOCAL LGBT NGOS

Legal environment

- Some difficulty registering NGOs in all countries. Registration does not appear to be possible in Belarus.
- Burdensome registration and reporting processes (e.g., Russian NGO law).
- Registration results in the increased potential for government attention, such as through audits.
- Fledgling local groups do not have the capacity to maintain NGO status.

Organizational capacity

- Most have a board of directors or advisors.
- Many use websites, blogs, and social media to reach out; some might have a Facebook page in place of a website.
- Understand the importance of discretion.
- Access to LGBT people in towns and rural areas is very limited.
- Most groups have few full-time staff; newer groups often have no paid staff.
- LGBT groups, especially those outside of large cities, depend on critical individuals to keep the groups active. Also, their small budgets mean that they do not have experience managing much funding.
- Most rely on volunteers for help, but some hire consultants or research organizations.
- Lack ability to fight off cyber-attacks.

Financial viability

- Most NGOs have a few sources of funding.
- A few NGOs have received USAID funding directly or via USAID implementers.
- Smaller NGOs receive grants from small funders.
- Majority of funding is project-based, but some general support funds are available.
- Organizations only receive funding from or channeled through government ministries for work related to HIV/AIDS.
- GFATM grants funds to sub-recipients that target MSM in each E&E country.
- Some NGOs are supported by international foundations that focus on or include LGBT rights in their portfolio (e.g., Hivos, Open Society Foundation, Arcus, and Astraea).
- A few NGOs have set up social enterprises, while others have charged fees for activities or services (see Davis, 2008 for case studies).

---

48. LGBT NGOs are not specifically mentioned in the 2011 CSO Sustainability Index for the E&E region and only briefly mentioned in the 2010 report. While there is not enough information available to do a full analysis, the framework will be used to categorize information gleaned from reports, NGO websites, and communication with activists in the region.

Advocacy

- It appears that most local and national LGBT NGOs do not have access to state structures or participate in decision-making and planning processes; the highest profile NGOs work with government.
- Smaller and fledgling NGOs are not able to design and implement programs that result in social change.
- Many tie their advocacy to EU accession and partnership agreements.
- NGOs communicate with EU, OSCE, and COE directly through press releases, letters, meetings/conferences, situation reports.
- NGOs run awareness raising campaigns and create flyers, posters, stickers; hold rallies and marches as well as innovative events such as flash mobs and bicycle rides; and they have radio shows.
- NGOs have found that coalition building and working with allies to include SOGI in the scope of public policy development is more successful when a non-LGBT ally takes the lead in the negotiations.
- Many do not collect the evidence that is needed for effective advocacy or policy design at multiple levels.

Service provision

- Clients are hard to identify and reach owing to stigma.
- Organizations rely on social media and word of mouth to attract clients.
- Extant client data is limited.
- National NGOs work throughout the country.
- Local NGOs focuses on city where based.
- Provide psychosocial support and legal assistance; some arrange cultural events and leisure activities.
- Run hotlines and support/self-help groups; host forums and chat areas on their websites.
- Share knowledge through website and information campaigns.
- Hold events for LGBT people (e.g., art exhibits, film festivals).
- It is not clear that there is a case management approach to helping clients.

Capacity to gather data

- Many organizations interview LGBT people and report on the results.
- Generally, a human rights framework informs documenting and reporting practices, guided by such documents as the Yogyakarta Principles (ICJ, 2007).
- Informants can be hard to locate. Transgender people may disappear into society and live in their gender after their gender reassignment surgery.
- LGBT people are leery of sharing information. Informants desire confidentiality and data safety, particularly those who compartmentalize their lives (e.g., those out to friends but not out to family/work). Also, the real possibility of police raids and cyber-attacks is worrisome. Police could require bribes to maintain secrecy.
- Questions arise as to how to collect, store, and analyze data.
- Most NGOs do not undertake quantitative data collection; if they do, data are often presented in an unclear manner.
- It is not clear that qualitative data collection is rigorous in most instances.
- A few organizations are able fund more rigorous data collection by external actors; fewer are able to fund it annually.
- Existing materials and reports are limited in breadth and depth.
- NGOs not collecting data on LGBT people in sectors of importance to USAID, including education, employment, human rights, gender, and health (except HIV/AIDS).
- Gathering in-depth data on occurrences and individual experiences in different contexts (e.g., rural/urban, workplace/school), and overall conditions for LGBT people in a manner that will be useful for later advocacy work is challenging.

Infrastructure

- Most NGOs are located in capital cities, some in other major cities; many in secret locations.
- Limited number of public meeting places in cities.
- More experienced organizations have branches or related groups in other cities; some local NGOs emerge from existing NGOs.
- Many fledgling groups in the region; national NGOs can facilitate contact with local grassroots NGOs.
- NGOs cooperate with other domestic LGBT organizations.
- The alliance that organizes the International Day Against Homophobia and Transphobia (IDAHO) has been active in the region, and has provided a point of focus and support for LGBT action.
- Few NGOs have allies, and informants attested to difficulty in coalescing and networking with organizations that are or could be allies.
- Allies work on gender issues, human rights, transparent governance, and HIV/AIDS.

Public image

- Organizations maintain a low physical profile, but most have an online presence.
- Work of local NGOs not very visible to public.
- Receive attention in relation to Gay Pride and IDAHO events; there have been violent attacks on events.
- Media coverage is uneven and sensational. It tends to incite violence rather than support.

Sources: Organizational Websites; communications with organizational representatives; Karmanau, 2013; GISH, 2006; van der Veur, 2007; Ivantchenko, 2010, Carroll & Quinn, 2009; Kohler, 2012; ILGA-Europe, 2011c; U.S. Department of State, 2008; Nash Mir 2007; IDAHO, n.d.; COWI & DIHR 2010a–k; personal communications. Kirichenko, Kseniya, 26 March 2012; personal communication Maymulakhin, Andriy, 11 March 2012; personal communication, Sabir, Kirill, 19 March 2012; GenderDoc-M, 2012; Carroll, 2010; ICNL, 2013; Davis, 2008

The most active and high-profile NGOs are located in Ukraine, Serbia, Russia, and Moldova. These four countries have a few well-established LGBT organizations that participate in coalitions of LGBT organizations. They also intercede with or advocate to state actors when needed. LGBT NGOs in the Republic of Macedonia, Georgia, and Bosnia and Herzegovina enjoy the support of larger organizations with whom they are affiliated. Armenia and Albania have a small number of recently established LGBT NGOs that have built significant civil society alliances. LGBT NGO activity in Azerbaijan and Montenegro appears to be more limited in scope. The three LGBT NGOs in Kosovo are all located in the capital (Savic, 2013). Appendix 8 contains a directory of LGBT organizations and allies by country.

Much of the work of LGBT organizations and coalitions at national, regional, and international levels—including those of the E&E region—focuses on the recognition and protection of human rights. The main pillars of LGBT advocacy in the region are:

- Challenging discrimination and encouraging the adoption of comprehensive anti-discrimination legislation.
- Criminalizing and calling attention to hate crimes and hate speech against LGBT people.
- Securing freedom of assembly for LGBT people and NGOs.
- Ensuring appropriate health care and timely identity registration for transgender people.
- Raising public awareness of the rights of LGBT people.
- Securing the inclusion of LGBT people in public and private institutions.

One component of NGO advocacy work in the region is the preparation of shadow reports for UN treaty bodies. These reports are often submitted in collaboration with international and regional LGBT and human rights organizations. The purpose of these reports is to reveal how well a government is complying with its obligations under international human rights frameworks and to highlight infringements. For example, reports to the Committee on the Elimination of Discrimination Against Women (CEDAW) highlight problems faced by women. Organizations may also submit background documents to be considered as stakeholder information by committees compiling reports. Appendix 9 is a matrix of shadow reports submitted by, with, or on behalf of LGBT NGOs.

Providing or arranging for safe spaces in which vulnerable or isolated LGBT people can come out, meet, share experiences, and support each other and have access to resources is also a key function for many groups in the region. Patterns of socializing indicate that while women, men, and transgender people may share some social spaces in the LGBT community, they also convene separately, reflecting their different experiences and types of support needed. Many LGBT NGOs create web-based publications, forums, and chat rooms as well as short run print publications that disseminate information of interest to their communities. Important to community cohesion, a number of better-established NGOs support grassroots LGBT groups directly and through coalitions, such as the LGBT Network in Russia and the Council of LGBT Organizations of Ukraine.[49]

Countering HIV/AIDS provides entrée to the LGBT community. Many of the LGBT NGOs in the region promote the prevention and treatment of HIV/AIDS and STIs, and they partner with HIV/AIDS-related service providers where possible. Providing information and education on sexual health is a means to reach and strengthen the LGBT community (AIDSTAR 2, 2010).

B. REGIONAL NGOS

Regional-level NGOs include national NGOs and coalitions. They also engage with international organizations and send representatives to international conferences. Regional NGOs include organizations such as the Eurasian Coalition on Male Health, Transgender Europe (TGEU),[50] ILGA-Europe, ARC International, COC Netherlands, and International Gay and Lesbian Youth Organisation (IGLYO). ILGA-Europe provides support, guidance, and models of good practice to LGBT groups around Europe (Peers, 2011, Polácek & Le Déroff, 2011, Polácek & Le Déroff, 2010, Loudes & Paradis, 2008). Since 2006, ILGA-Europe has implemented programs such as Prevention and Empowerment in the CIS (PRECIS) and study visits to OSCE, CoE, and EU institutions for representatives of LGBT organizations in Armenia, Azerbaijan, Georgia, Moldova, and Ukraine (ILGA-Europe, 2011f). They have, or in the case of newer organizations, are planning for, boards of advisors and board elections, steering committees, secretariats, membership processes, websites, and social media outreach. These NGOs seek additional funding from sources other than the UN or bilateral donors. They advocate for support of target groups; provide training on advocacy; hold events; ensure representation of their target groups in international conferences, organizations, and advisory councils; and hold gatherings of representatives of NGOs serving target groups. They also serve as information resources for LGBT people and organizations via websites and social media. In addition, regional NGOs support the collection of data on LGBT people and serve as a conduit for sharing information about the situation of LGBT people in the E&E region with national governments, the EU, UN, and international organizations.

C. ALLIES

Partnership with allies and networks is particularly important for LGBT NGOs in the region as they allow organizations to find common ground and learn about each other's issues. Allies include donors and partners who work in areas such as gender issues, HIV/AIDS, and human rights. In terms of advocacy, allies help legitimize claims, develop skills, and access networks that interface with state bodies.

Regional and national donors provide project-level support. These donors include the Ukrainian Women's Fund, EU and U.S. Embassies, Open Society Foundations, International Renaissance Foundation, Remembrance, Responsibility and Future Foundation, Trag Foundation for Community Initiatives (Serbia), and the Sigrid Rausing Trust. They provide small-grants assistance with projects related to human rights as well as hate crime monitoring and victim counseling.

National and local NGOs that work with LGBT NGOs include the Helsinki Committees for Human Rights in multiple countries as well as other human rights defenders and organizations working on HIV/AIDS. In Georgia and Kosovo,[51] Helsinki Committees, and the Helsinki Association in Armenia, advocated for the human rights of LGBT people before any LGBT organizations were set up in the countries.

---

49. It was not possible to further describe the All-Ukrainian Union "Council of LGBT Organisations of Ukraine," which does not have a website or make information about the organization available online. However, it was found that 19 organizations are members (Maimulakhin, A., 2011).

50. Transgender Europe (TGEU), the first pan-European transgender organization that supports transgender activists in the E&E region, was established in 2005.

51. The Helsinki Committee for Human Rights in Serbia is active in Kosovo.

Organizations that focus on health or human rights usually designate one or two individuals with access to the institutional expertise and resources of the parent NGO to work on LGBT issues. It has been reported that human rights defenders who work on LGBT issues have faced isolation and attacks on their non-LGBT-related work (Carroll and Quinn, 2009). Generally, organizations working with LGBT NGOs share information and provide services that LGBT NGOs do not have the capacity to provide, such as legal representation for clients, helping with hate crime data analysis, and voicing support in public fora. In regard to HIV/AIDS and service providers, NGOs and umbrella organizations partner with LGBT NGOs to reach MSM, WSW, and transgender people. (See Appendix 7 for information on groups allied with LGBT people).

VI. RECOMMENDATIONS

The scale of the work needed to address the challenges facing LGBT people cannot be overestimated. The path forward for USAID likely requires internal policies and guidance on addressing issues important to LGBT people and integrating them into USAID programming. Facilitating more rigorous research, data collection, and well-informed program design can help USAID and implementing partners engage LGBT people and NGOS and the challenges they face. Evidence-based policymaking and programming begins with research into the difficulties facing USAID LGBT programming.

A. POTENTIAL CHALLENGES AND OBSTACLES TO USAID LGBT PROGRAMMING IN THE E&E REGION

International NGOs such as ILGA-Europe and COC Netherlands have provided substantial and meaningful support to national LGBT NGOs in the region. USAID's new emphasis on working with LGBT NGOs and addressing LGBT issues in the region puts it in the company of the Swedish International Development Agency (SIDA). Challenges ahead include:

- Hostility to outside influence and intervention by a variety of national actors;
- Stigmatization of LGBT people and organizations;
- The widespread belief that human rights covenants and anti-discrimination laws do not apply to sexual orientation or gender identity;
- Public perception that LGBT people's needs are inappropriate for public discussion or policy-making;
- LGBT people fear exposure to hostile elements in society;
- Possible attempts to politicize certain USAID programs by media, local politicians, anti-LGBT activists, and religious figures, particularly those dealing with children;
- Possible difficulty engaging civil service actors such as service providers in health, education, law enforcement, and the judiciary on LGBT issues as a result of their intolerance of LGBT people;
- Rejection of LGBT integration by partner and beneficiary organizations;
- The need to monitor the behavior of individual and NGO participants toward LGBT participants in order to ensure a welcoming, non-discriminatory environment;
- Individuals and groups could target participants, partners, or USAID staff members and their physical offices, training sites, or events for disruption or violence.

B. SPECIFIC RECOMMENDATIONS

STRENGTHEN USAID KNOWLEDGE AND CAPACITY FOR LGBT ENGAGEMENT
These recommendations concern preparing USAID to integrate SOGI-related matters into its work.

Develop USAID-generated guidance. To ensure a uniform and measurable standard in processes and approaches to addressing issues of importance to LGBT persons and including them in USAID programming, more comprehensive policy and implementation guidance is needed. For example, a policy or strategy could be developed that lays out how to work with LGBT people and addresses issues of importance to them throughout the program cycle; relevant requirements could be integrated in USAID's Automated Directive System (ADS); and help documents could be authored that facilitate an understanding of the policy and ADS. Guidance could also be developed which outlines the linguistic norms to be followed when working with LGBT people. USAID does anticipate finalizing its draft vision document (similar to a policy) by the end of 2013.

It may be necessary to develop standard monitoring and evaluation indicators that reflect LGBT inclusion and engagement (cf., USAID's standard indicators for gender). Toolkits might be needed to help Missions and USAID/Washington staff develop project and activity level indicators for measuring how projects have met needs of LGBT people and closed gaps where they are disadvantaged compared to the heterosexual population. USAID staff could benefit from guidance on how to attribute spending on LGBT-related work when reporting on gender-related budget allocations in Operational Plans and on LGBT-related results in annual Performance Plans and Reports (PPRs).

Currently USAID disaggregates data by biological sex, which doesn't reflect how all transgender people want to be identified—some reject male/female labels entirely. Attention is needed to determine how to address this issue in relation to USAID's work.

In addition to central policies, USAID Missions could develop language for Mission Orders (MOs) that describe how Missions will engage with and include LGBT people in programming. This could be integrated into MOs dealing with vulnerable groups or gender. It is also important to consider the vulnerability of LGBT youth when planning for youth engagement and inclusion in programming. MOs can also detail the role of USAID as a visible ally to LGBT communities, as a participant in events, and as a partner with other donors (e.g., EU, CoE, and OSCE). As a separate action, Missions can determine their role and the role of their implementers if it comes to their attention that a LGBT person is in imminent danger.

Sample Indicators:
- Number of strategy and policy documents in place.
- Comprehensive implementation guidance in place (yes/no).
- Appropriate requirements related to integrating LGBT people included in the ADS (yes/no).
- Annual reporting occurs to track USAID's work with LGBT populations (when it can be done without endangering anyone) (yes/no).
- Number of regional Missions with strategies for engaging and addressing the needs of LGBT people integrated into MOs for all regional Missions.

Build USAID/Washington and Mission staff's knowledge of LGBT people and NGOs and methods for engaging them in the E&E region. E&E-specific guidance for integrating attention to LGBT issues and engaging LGBT people is needed. Mission and USAID/Washington champions could work together with gender advisors in the Missions and the E&E Bureau to compile informational materials and develop training exercises to introduce Mission staff to LGBT inclusion and sensitivity in project design. A section on the E&E Bureau's Social Transition Team website could be designated as a repository for relevant documents. Such efforts could involve LGBT activists and human rights defenders. Staff could learn about such topics as:

- The distinction between sexual orientation and gender identity;
- Issues faced by gay men, lesbians, bisexual men and women, and transgender men and women in different age groups;
- Agency policy and local laws that could affect the inclusion of LGBT people in programming;
- LGBT NGOs' approaches to advocacy;
- Personal prejudice regarding homosexuality, including how to address one's hidden biases and discomfort related to working with or supporting LGBT people;
- Methods and practices that enable the safe inclusion of LGBT people in programming targeted at a wider audience; and
- Other donors' work in this area and avoiding duplication of efforts.

> **Resource**
> The International Planned Parenthood Federation developed a toolkit that includes (a) a survey for measuring staff and provider attitudes and knowledge about working with people with diverse sexual orientations and gender identities, (b) indicators useful for planning service provision and advocacy, and (c) an index to assess agency readiness (IPPF, 2005).

Sample Indicators:
- Number of times LGBT issues are included in analyses and documents related to project design and procurement.
- Percentage of press releases that indicate understanding of the issues.
- Number of knowledge-sharing sites hosting information on LGBT issues that is relevant to USAID.

INCREASE THE INTEGRATION OF LGBT PERSPECTIVES IN THE DESIGN OF PROJECTS AND STRATEGIES

LGBT Champions. E&E Missions could encourage LGBT champions to lead discussions on best practices and strategies to integrate LGBT NGOs and LGBT individuals in USAID sectoral and cross-cutting programming. Champions could also identify informants who can be recommended and engaged by Missions to share knowledge and obtain feedback relevant to current and future programming.

Sample Indicators:
- Number of Missions with LGBT champions.
- Number of briefings by LGBT champions and level of attendance.

CDCS and project-level analysis. Required gender analyses as well as optional youth and vulnerable group analyses could integrate questions on LGBT people and issues. Appendix 5 suggests sample questions for this inclusive analysis. Questions on LGBT issues could also be integrated into other assessments, including labor market, community serving organizations, value chain, education, and anti-corruption. Organizations currently collect information according to the rights laid out in such documents as the Yogyakarta Principles (ICH, 2007). Some of this information is relevant to USAID work and could serve as a useful starting point for research related to education, rule of law, labor market participation, social assistance, combatting human trafficking, health, civil society, governance, and media.

Sample Indicators:
- Number of consultations with LGBT champions during project design.
- Number of analyses and assessments that include discussions of lesbians, gay men, bisexuals, and transgender people.
- Number of CDCSs, project appraisal documents, assessments, and solicitations that integrate LGBT issues.

Research and development of indicators to be used in monitoring and evaluation. It is essential that groups across the LGBT spectrum be included in research for indicator design so that the final product is as comprehensive as possible. Research can draw on indicators developed for work with vulnerable groups and gender-sensitive indicators. For cross-cutting projects or projects in areas where barriers to LGBT people have been identified (e.g., participation in the labor market), it may be necessary to develop indicators for exploring multiple aspects of the situation. For example, it would be desirable to look at both the level of employment of LGBT people and their experiences of discrimination. Also, looking at the Standard USAID Indicators for Gender-Based Violence (GBV) from an LGBT perspective might help determine their applicability to projects aimed at preventing or responding to violence against LGBT people.

In order to ascertain how well projects include LGBT people and whether they achieve positive outcomes, indicators need to be developed to measure (a) engagement (level and quality of participation), (b) project outputs (e.g., number of laws passed, service providers trained, access to facilities increased), and (c) outcomes or impacts (e.g., have health care providers been providing better services or are employers enforcing new human resources policies). Indicators can help USAID see if gaps between LGBT people and the heterosexual population have been affected by the project.

Confidentiality and data security. Information gathering must be voluntary and confidential. It must be offered freely and obtained in a way that does not require the public identification of a person's sexual orientation or status as a MSM/WSW. While it is possible that certain NGOs and individuals might be more likely to self-select for participation in certain types of projects (e.g., projects that focus on civil society capacity building, decreasing violent behavior among youth, or preventing HIV/AIDS), individuals must not be required to self-identify in order to do so. The development and application of data safety protocols can encourage people to report personal and confidential information. Data need to be "de-identified" (names and other unique information are replaced with code), and safeguards for data storage need to be in place to prevent access by people other than project implementers and researchers.

Strategic data collection and analysis. If possible, it might be useful to cross-tabulate by different characteristics when analyzing data. Doing so will help researchers identify instances of multiple discrimination and determine whether projects need to address certain factors. Depending on the type of program, different data on life experiences, behaviors, and knowledge can be collected and compared. For example, a pre- and post-intervention survey on life skill development and workforce participation could include questions that allow for analysis by age group, sex, information on SOGI, disability status, ethnicity, and HIV/AIDS status.

Sample Indicators:
- Number of reliable LGBT-sensitive indicators used in project design, implementation, and monitoring and evaluation documents.
- Number of reports completed that detail the results of measuring such indicators.

35

- Number of confidential data collection and storage requirements that are in place and followed.
- Number of staff trained in collecting data from LGBT populations.
- Number of analyses that look at disaggregated data to determine how lesbian, gay, bisexual, and transgender people are differentially affected by gender and other issues.
- Number of diagnostics (e.g., surveys and interview protocols) being used that allow staff to determine where to focus efforts when working with those who could experience multiple discrimination.

CREATE OPPORTUNITIES FOR SUSTAINED ENGAGEMENT WITH LGBT NGOS AND ACTIVISTS

Most LGBT NGOs in the region have not worked with USAID or other bilateral donors. They will need orientation, training, and assistance to engage with USAID Missions and projects. To begin, Mission staff could identify and invite LGBT leaders to the Mission to begin a dialogue that would help them map the NGO landscape and learn more about activists, the NGOs, their work, and how they collaborate. This circle of informants could be expanded to include activists and individuals in smaller and non-registered organizations. It is important that NGOs and activists understand the difference between USAID and United Nations Development Programme (UNDP), United Nations Population Fund (UNFPA), the EU, and CoE. This is important because USAID is an international development agency that is held closely accountable by the U.S. Congress and taxpayers and has projects in multiple sectors, while the UN and European organizations engage LGBT people in fewer sectors, such as health, human rights monitoring, and civil society development.

Standing LGBT working groups. In order to inform USAID programming across Mission portfolios and throughout the program cycle, a standing working group could be created. Depending on participant availability and Mission needs, some members could meet face-to-face while others could provide feedback virtually. While the groups would likely start out as USAID-only, they could be expanded to include LGBT champions among implementers, international LGBT NGO representatives in-country, local LGBT NGO representatives, and local allies. Such working groups should include lesbian, gay, bisexual, and transgender individuals.

It would be useful to facilitate networking and information sharing among such working groups across the E&E region. Members could meet and share information virtually with an eye toward helping USAID staff ensure that programming is responding to and engaging LGBT people. Network members could work together to help USAID set up systems to protect individual LGBT project participants, similar to one employed in Ghana where allies in positions of authority were trained to identify and report abuse to implementing partners who could deploy trained lawyers to provide assistance (USAID, n.d.).

Sample Indicators:
- Number of established working groups.
- Number of regular working group meetings.
- Number of networking events held or websites created.
- Level of inclusiveness of the working group—do members include lesbians, gay men, bisexuals, transgender people, straight people, men and women, and ethnic minorities.
- Number of working groups engaged in helping USAID set up and monitor systems used to engage and protect LGBT beneficiaries.
- Number of incidents where working group advice has influenced project design, monitoring, and evaluation.
- Number of events or knowledge-sharing activities held.
- Level of participant satisfaction with their working group (measured using a Likert scale).

BUILD LGBT NGOS' CAPACITY AS CIVIL SOCIETY ACTORS

Informants from Ukraine, Belarus, Albania, and elsewhere affirm that assistance with strengthening NGOs and CSOs as well as LGBT community capacity building is very important in the E&E region. This set of recommendations focuses on enhancing LGBT organizations' stability, operational capacity, and policy work. The list is not exhaustive and the importance of individual recommendations will vary from country to country. Key areas of work need to be determined with LGBT NGOs and their allies.

Organizational capacity. Building organizational capacity will require training and mentoring. Seminars and webinars such as those provided by InsideNGO and the Center for Development Excellence can be adapted to this audience or they could be linked to other training providers.[52] Trainings like these, which include strategic planning, accounting, financial management, human resources, and rules and regulations, will be important for NGOs that wish to grow. Financial and management capacity audits done by projects issuing sub-grants can be a key tool for assessing an organization's ability to manage funds and a source of organizational learning. Since the region has both established high profile organizations and fledgling startups, and USAID supports programs that offer a variety of grants, these audits can help determine which groups might be ready for larger grants and which are better suited for small or micro-grants. Both training and audits can contribute to the sustainability of USAID's impact.

Diversifying funding sources. Entering into innovative funding arrangements can bring LGBT NGOs closer to each other as well as local and international LGBT communities. LGBT activists or successful start-ups from outside the region who are familiar with crowdsourcing funds via platforms like Kickstarter and Crowdrise could be encouraged to provide training. Another area to explore would be connecting LGBT organizations with information and training on founding and running online and brick-and-mortar social enterprises. Such enterprises exist in Moldova as well as Russia and Romania.[53] Lessons learned could be sought from LGBT NGOs who have opened social enterprises in the E&E region and shared with potential entrepreneurs who could receive mentoring and support from USAID partners.

Improving Data Collection. Increased research capacity is essential to provide LGBT NGOs with a more detailed picture of their clientele, as well as human rights ombudsmen and allies with actionable evidence to affect law and policy. International donors and organizations also need a clear picture of how they can contribute to improving the situation. Research is needed in a variety of areas. As with any in-depth research with marginalized or vulnerable populations, such as domestic violence or HIV/AIDS-related research, research methods involving LGBT people in the E&E region must be sensitive to respondents' safety and privacy, and that of the researchers. The following activities could be considered:

- Training LGBT NGOs on the basics of data collection, the kind of evidence needed for advocacy, research methods for collecting qualitative and quantitative data from vulnerable populations, data analysis, and presentation.

- Helping LGBT NGOs connect with social science researchers capable of reaching vulnerable populations who can collect, analyze, and present data without bias, and provide training in effectively documenting rights violations in different sectors.

- Supporting NGO efforts to set up hotlines and text message platforms to collect data. Consider using platforms such as Ushahidi open source software for data collection, visualization, and interactive mapping, which has been used to crowdmap human rights issues around the world (both online and via mobile phone), including election violations in Ukraine and Moldova and violence against women and girls in the Republic of Macedonia (Ushahidi.com, 2013).

- Commissioning LGBT country situation reports that require the use of a standardized methodology and unified structure that facilitates comparative analysis.

- Requiring data safety training and a security plan aimed at ensuring the safety of informants and data collectors when USAID funds data collection.

Alliances. In order to increase the sustainability of investments in LGBT NGOs, USAID could facilitate and encourage their collaboration with other beneficiaries of USAID programming, as well as their participation in regional networks and cross-border collaboration mechanisms. The Eurasian Coalition on Male Health (ECOM), for example, received assistance with knowledge-sharing and capacity building from UNDP and the GFTAM in the form of an inter-regional meeting with the Asia Pacific Coalition on Male Sexual Health (Global Forum on MSM & HIV, 2011). While it is not often possible to support regional or extra-regional conferences and workshops, implementers could use methods such as study tours, bringing in trainers from other countries in the region, and online collaboration to encourage alliances. Cross-border collaboration might be possible since human rights

---

52. For the kinds of trainings offered, see: https://www.insidengo.org/events/ and http://www.cderesources.com/

53. For more information, see Davis, 2008.

defenders and LGBT activists already communicate across borders. The role USAID might play has yet to be defined but could include working with global development partners to encourage fellowship across the region.

Support community cohesion. USAID has supported certain aspects of shelter services and community centers. It is clear that the LGBT community needs safe spaces to meet and seek refuge. However, further exploration is needed to see where and how the kinds of services USAID might fund could work in the security context faced by organizations, and what additional funding sources would be needed. As in past efforts to assist vulnerable groups, USAID support could integrate other services with the shelter model, such as workforce readiness and entrepreneurship training and micro-credit.

Sample Indicators:
- Proportion of LGBT activists and NGOs that:
    - Participate in financial and management training.
    - Demonstrate increased organizational capacity.
    - Join and maintain membership in national, regional networks and actively participate in network activities.
    - Use online funding platforms.
    - Participate in social enterprise development and management training.
    - Start social enterprises and proportion that remain in business a year later.
    - Provide workforce readiness training, psycho-social support, and legal assistance.
- Number of LGBT NGOs that exhibit the ability to sustain and grow their level of activity as a result of capacity building activities.
- Number of for-profit social enterprises run by LGBT NGOs and activists that are able to invest in social causes or expand their service delivery.
- Proportion of data available from trained NGOs that was gathered using rigorous methods.
    - Amount of data that is comparable across years and countries.
- Number of instances data demonstrably influenced interventions by NGOs and activists.
- Number of leadership roles in networks taken by beneficiary organizations and activists.
- Number of community centers funded without donor assistance.

Support LGBT NGOs' efforts to advocate for change and protect human rights. Currently, all Mission portfolios in the E&E region include some focus on strengthening civil society organizations' capability to advocate as well as plan, monitor, and evaluate their activities. Many LGBT NGOs need training and mentoring in advocacy and awareness raising in areas such as branding and strategizing, political engagement, preparing for meeetings with decision-makers and media, writing effective reports, designing information campaigns, using Information Communication Technology (ICTs) for more effective and innovative advocacy, and developing focused and efficient coalitions and partnerships. LGBT NGOs also need training in constituency building, which in addition to the above skills, includes courting and developing allies, networking, reaching out to hard-to-reach populations, and activating constituents.

Reports indicate that LGBT NGOs would value additional training in human rights and support for the design and production of awareness raising materials and targeted outreach activities. Key target groups include health care providers; government officials; civil servants responsible for identity documents; police and judges; teachers and administrators of educational institutions; and private sector business owners and managers. In addition to support for making an effective human rights case, training could also be provided in making a compelling business case—clarifying the benefits of making an investment—for respecting an individual's human rights regardless of sexual orientation or gender identity.

Sample Indicators:
- Number of LGBT NGOs that:
    - Undertake awareness-raising campaigns.
    - Have strategies for advocacy and implement them.
    - Use innovative means to reach the public, including ICTs.
    - Report meetings with government officials.
    - Increase the number of volunteers mobilized for events and other activities.
    - Reach out to private firms to encourage tolerance of LGBT employees.

38

- Are able to connect with hard-to-reach populations.
- Train target groups (e.g., police) in tolerance.
- Number of citizens who report decreased negative feelings about LGBT people in opinion surveys.
- Number of government officials who report supporting LGBT rights who were reached out to by LGBT NGOs and activists.
- Decreased number of negative portrayals of LGBT people in films, television, and print media.
- Increased number of allied organizations available for partnership and collaboration.

INCLUDE LGBT PEOPLE AND NGOS IN OTHER USAID PROGRAMMING

Cross-cutting issues. Efforts in women's empowerment and gender equality, youth engagement, empowering people with disabilities, and supporting the integration of ethnic minorities could be elaborated by including efforts to identify and address multiple discrimination.

Health. USAID's health systems strengthening activities could integrate activities focused on improving the healthcare experience of gay, lesbian, bisexual, and especially transgender people. Activities could work to improve management of care, health governance, leadership, and information systems; smooth a transgender person's transition process; and build the capacity of providers to deliver quality services in an unbiased manner to everyone in the LGBT community.

Because few countries in the E&E region continue to fund HIV/AIDS-related work, it is important that current USAID projects continue to fund work with MSM and sex workers in larger and smaller cities.

> "As development professionals, our actions and work must reflect the values of democracy, human rights and inclusion. Our Agency has been instrumental in advancing these principles for LGBT communities. All of our efforts—from HIV/AIDS programs to humanitarian assistance—are based on principles of nondiscrimination and equitable access."
>
> –Rajiv Shah, 2013

Social protection. In partnership with other donors, USAID could provide capacity building support to NGOs and LGBT leaders in areas such as case management (ensuring that people receive the services they need), service provision, and creating economic opportunities. This work can be adapted from best practices and lessons learned in work with other vulnerable groups. This capacity building work will be especially relevant to psycho-social service providers.

Education. USAID education programming could integrate LGBT sensitivity training into work with teachers and administrators and promote the protection of LGBT students attending partner higher education institutions. In addition, youth engagement, workforce development, life skills training, and leadership programs could work with LGBT NGOs to identify and engage young LGBT youth.

Governance and rule of law. USAID could support efforts to help judges, prosecutors, and legal professionals learn new areas of law and increase effectiveness in prosecuting anti-discrimination laws.

Media. Many LGBT NGOs are using blogs to communicate. USAID could include bloggers on LGBT issues in capacity building and networking activities.

Economic growth. Business development and competitiveness initiatives could include education and training to counter the negative effects of homophobia in the workplace as well as discussion of how they affect a company's productivity. Efforts to strengthen human resources could introduce the concept of LGBT people as a protected class in the workplace and work on related employee policies.

Sample Indicators:
- Number of partnerships of LGBT organizations with women's and disabled people's organizations.
- Number of medical staff (doctors, nurses, administrators) trained in healthcare for LGBT people.
    - Number of LGBT people reporting improved treatment and bedside manner of trained medical staff.
- Number of health care facilities with policies in place regarding the treatment of LGBT people.

- Number of health care facilities that demonstrate the capacity to ensure a pleasant experience for LGBT people.
- Proportion of schools and universities that have or put policies in place to promote tolerance of LGBT students.
  - Number of LGBT student groups established.
- Number of trained teachers and administrators at all levels who report not tolerating discrimination based on their sexual orientation and gender identity in their institutions.
- Number of LGBT youth engaged in workforce development and entrepreneurship training programs.
  - Number of LGBT youth who report finding permanent employment or become self-employed in the formal sector as a result of training.
- Number of judges, prosecutors, and legal professional who receive training on the protection of the rights of LGBT people under anti-discrimination laws.
- Number of human resources and executive staff of businesses participating in economic growth programming who are presented with the business case for not tolerating homophobia and transphobia in the workplace.
  - Number of their staff of who receive training in tolerance.
- Number of LGBT employees of businesses participating in economic growth programming who report increased tolerance.

In the E&E region, LGBT people are struggling to achieve recognition and protection of their human rights. Several E&E Missions are actively supporting programming that addresses LGBT issues through numerous approaches and others have done so in the past or are hoping to do so in the near future. To join the LGBT Champions List, contact DCHA.

APPENDIX 1: LANGUAGE USE REGARDING LGBT PEOPLE IN THE E&E REGION

A Russian-speaking informant, with inputs from others, describes how local languages refer to LGBT people in the region. Except to clarify the English translation, their voices have been left largely intact.

LESBIAN, GAY AND BISEXUAL PEOPLE

The most negative and offensive terms relating to LGB people: «пидор» (pidor), «пидорас» (pederast), «педик» (pedik); "gomik" (homo) or "gyot" (a word of Turkish origin meaning "bum," equivalent to "faggot" — a gay man); «лезбуха» (lesbucka — lesbian). Various words for "pervert" are common across the region.

More neutral, but also with negative connotations: «розовые» (rozovye, literally "pink" —lesbian) and «голубые» (golubye, literally "light blue" — gay men) are more archaic words, but still present. «пидовка» (pidovka) is a negative word, but is more often used by gay men themselves and has become slang. The words "faggot" and "queer" are used derogatorily in Macedonia and across the western Balkans.

The terms «мужеложство» (muzhelozhstvo) and «мужеложник» (muzhelozhnik) initially referred to gay men in Russian Orthodox religious discourse, but were used also in criminal law when criminalizing same-sex voluntary or involuntary relations before decriminalization of homosexuality in 1993 in Russia. They are still used now, something like "sodomy" in English.

There are also interesting words like «гомосексуализм» (gomoseksualizm), «бисексуализм» (biseksualizm), «гомосексуалист» (gomoseksualist), and «бисексуалист» (biseksualist). What is interesting here is that these terms were used before ICD-10 in relation to medical diagnosis. The suffix "-izm/-ist" usually means either disease or ideology.

Many LGBT people and especially LGBT activists and gender researchers ask people to abstain from using these words because of their negative connotations. Instead of this, they recommend that the neutral words «гомосексуальность» (gomoseksualnost — homosexuality) and «гомосексуал» (gomoseksual — homosexual) be used.

What is also interesting, in contrast to English discourse, in the Russian language most LGBT people, LGBT activists and even researchers, do not question the appropriateness of words like "homosexual" vs. expressions like "homosexual person" or even "gay people."

Finally, the most appropriate and neutral terms are «гомосексуал» (gomoseksual), «гей» (gey), «лесбиянка» (lesbiyanka), and «бисексуал» (biseksual). But sometimes lesbian women prefer not to name themselves using «лесбиянка» and prefer instead terms like «гомосексуальная женщина» (gomoseksualnaya zhenschina — "homosexual woman").

TRANSGENDER PEOPLE

Most of the terms are abbreviations and formed from English words, sometimes with added female endings typical for the Russian language. Thus, there are often used by representatives of trans community terms such as «мтф» (MtF), «фтм» (FtM), «ТС» (TS), «пре-опка»/«пре-оп» (pre-opka/pre-op), «пост-опка»/«пост-оп» (post-opka/post-op), «нон-опка»/«нон-оп» (non-opka/non-op). These terms are neutral.

In some groups, although less common, specific terms like «утка» (utka — a MtF person) are used. Some people use terms «транс» (trans), «трансы» (transy) that could be considered negative, especially by MtF persons.

Also negative in character are such terms as «трапы» (trapy), «трансухи» (transuhi), «членодевки» (chlenodevki), and «шимэйлы» (shimejly). However, the perception of such words very often depends on each concrete person; they could be neutral or even jokey if they are used by transgender persons in relation to other transgender person.

There is much misuse and interchangeability of the terms transgender, transsexual and transvestite in public and official environments across the E&E region. This suggests a confusion or misunderstanding of the separate realities and life implications of each of these populations. Further, the negative terms related to gays and lesbians are often used interchangeably for transgender and transsexual people, as many people in society do not understand the distinction between sexual orientation and gender identity. "Persons of a non-standard sexual orientation" —a commonly used misnomer for transgender people—denotes an assumed gay, lesbian, or bisexual orientation in the transgender person, which inaccurately categorizes them.

OFFICIAL USAGE

In current anti-propaganda legislation the following terms are used: «гомосексуализм» (gomoseksualizm — homosexualizm), «мужеложство» (muzhelozhstvo — sodomy), «лесбиянство» (lesbiyanstvo — lesbianism), «бисексуализм» (biseksualizm — bisexualism), and «трансгендерность» (transgendernost — transgenderness).

The Russian Criminal Code (Article 32 on "Violent Sexual Acts") and equivalent codes elsewhere use the terms «мужеложство» (muzhelozhstvo — sodomy) and «лесбиянство» (lesbiyanstvo — lesbianism). In Armenia the word "homo-addict" is frequently referred to.

The internationally recognized status of sexual orientation translates as "sex direction" in Macedonia, thereby rendering its legal meaning ambiguous. The term "sexual minorities" is widely referred to in the region, but is loosely defined.

Some regional by-laws describing programs on HIV/AIDS or STI prevention and sexual crime prevention also use the term «гомосексуалисты» (gomoseksualisty — homosexualists). The same words are the most common in public political speech. Some politicians sometimes use offensive terms such as «розовые» (rozovye), «голубые» (golubye), «педики» (pediki), or «содомиты» (sodomity).

The neutral terms such as «гомосексуал» (gomoseksual), «гей» (gey), or «бисексуал» (biseksual) are not, with very rare exceptions, used in official documents.

In relation to transsexual people in medical discourse and relevant orders from the Russian Ministry of Health, the term «транссексуализм» (transseksualizm) is used.

APPENDIX 2: PUBLIC ATTITUDES TOWARD LGBT PEOPLE IN NINE COUNTRIES IN THE E&E REGION

ATTITUDES SURVEYED AND % OF RESPONDENTS WHO AGREE

Country	Sample size	Homosexuality is illness / sin / disease	Homosexual relations are bad	Intolerant	Negative attitude to LGBT %	No to working with LGBT %	No to LGBT neighbor %	No to LGBT friend	No to LGBT family member	Social acceptance bad	Homosexuals should not be allowed to marry	No to LGBT raising children	Society/church should punish LGBT %	State should fight against / criminalize LGBT %
Armenia (Pink Armenia, 2011c)	1,156	18.6		49.6	72.1		86.5						66.9	77.5
Azerbaijan (Far Center, 2009—posted on 3rd View in 2010)	1,000 (18–30)				73									
Bosnia and Herzegovina (Durkovic, 2008)	1,550									76.7				
Bosnia and Herzegovina (Gallup Balkan Monitor) 2012	2,426				73.7									
Bosnia and Herzegovina (Gallup Balkan Monitor) 2011	1,009				74.6									
Bosnia and Herzegovina (Gallup Balkan Monitor) 2010	1,000				76.6									
Georgia (Quinn, 2007)	430	60*			84									
Georgia (Caucasus Research Resource Centers, as cited in Quinn, 2007)	not known					71.4	81.4							
Moldova (Soros Foundation-Moldova, 2010)	1,200		81		68	81	80	85	92~			77#	56	
Montenegro (Besic, M., 2011)	1,040						57							
Human Rights Action, 2009**	814	70.5									84.1	87.8	66.5†	58.1
Russia Levada Center, 2013	1,600	34									85^	62#		67∞
Russia Public Opinion Foundation, 2006	1,500	13.1			47									
Russian Public Opinion Research Center, 2005	1,600											59	67	
Serbia (Vukovic, Colovic, & Mojsilovic, 2008)	967	70**				47	38	64	70		90	95	60	51
Ukraine														

Country	Sample size	Homosexuality is illness / sin / disease	Homosexual relations are bad	Intolerant	Negative attitude to LGBT %	No to working with LGBT %	No to LGBT neighbor %	No to LGBT friend	No to LGBT family member	Social acceptance bad	Homosexuals should not be allowed to marry	No to LGBT raising children	Society/church should punish LGBT %	State should fight against / criminalize LGBT %
Ukraine Gorshenin Institute, 2011	1,000				72~~									
Ukraine (Nash Mir, 2011)														
Ukraine 2011	1,200										64	69		
Ukraine 2007	1,200										63	60		
Ukraine 2002	1,200										54	49		

Notes:
Year data collected matches publication year unless otherwise noted. No data for Albania, Belarus, Kosovo, and Republic of Macedonia.
* Lesbian only
~ Refers to "hav[ing] a family member marry a gay or lesbian" and not to blood relatives.
# No to adopting
^ Categories of sharply negative and rather negative included
∞ This percentage is the sum of positive and rather positive responses to the question, "What is your attitude toward the discussion in the State Duma of the law banning homosexual propaganda?" Sixty percent of respondents believe that the law was adopted because of concern for society's morality.
† Yes answer to "The Church is rightfully against homosexuality."
** Also in Table 2 in the main text
~~ Of the respondents, 57.5% answered that they had an entirely negative viewpoint of sexual minorities and 14.5% had a rather negative point of view.

The following table provides more information on a variety of opinions in Montenegro and Serbia. Similar questions were asked in Serbia in 2008 by the Gay Straight Alliance and the Centre for Free Elections and Democracy and in Montenegro in 2008 by Human Rights Action and Ipsos Strategic Marketing. Data showed that respondents in both countries supported the right to privately express sexual orientation, though public expression was viewed negatively. Respondents in Montenegro were generally more positive in their responses. Changes to the questions used in the surveys in Serbia between 2008 and 2010 could have affected responses.

PUBLIC ATTITUDES TOWARD LGBT PEOPLE IN MONTENEGRO AND SERBIA

Public attitudes	% of respondents who agree Montenegro 2009 N=814	% of respondents who agree Serbia 2008 N=967	% of respondents who agree Serbia 2010 N=1,405
Homosexuality is a disease	70.5	70	67
Homosexuality is an inherent characteristic	46.8		
Homosexuals are people like everyone else	60.2	38	52
Homosexuality is western invention in order to destroy a family*	28.9	36	38
Homosexuality always existed, before it was hidden and today one talks about it	86.9	67	67
Everyone has a right to his/her sexual orientation unless endangering others	89.4	65	67
Homosexuality is very dangerous for the society	57.6	50	56
The problem of homosexuality is unnecessarily being imposed by various NGOs**	42.5	28	47
The Church is rightfully against homosexuality	66.5	60	64
The state institutions should work on the suppression of homosexuality	58.1	51	53
If a political party I like would start advocating the rights of homosexuals I would discontinue voting for it	39.1	40	
There should be public places for socializing of homosexuals (clubs, bars)	37.6	22	23
Homosexuals are endangered minority and should be helped to achieve their rights	21.6	12	15
Homosexuals should be allowed to marry	15.9	10	14
Homosexuals should be allowed to register their partnership	20.9		
Gay parades are a legitimate way of peaceful gathering for promotion of the rights of homosexuals	20.7	8	12
Homosexuals should be allowed to adopt children	12.2	5	8

Notes:
* Question from 2010: Homosexuality was fabricated in the West, with the aim of destroying the family and our tradition.
** Question from 2010: The problem of homosexuality is imposed by various non-governmental organizations who make money on that.
Sources: Human Rights Action, 2009; Vukovic, Colovic, & Mojsilovic, 2008; GSA & CESID, 2010

APPENDIX 3: DISCRIMINATORY BEHAVIOR AGAINST LGBT PEOPLE IN FOUR COUNTRIES IN THE REGION

Type of behavior	Ukraine (LGBT Human Rights Nash Mir Center, 2013a) N=499 (MF)	Moldova (GenderDoc-M 2011a) N=220 (LGBT)	Bosnia and Herzegovina (Durkovic, 2008) N=210 (LGBTIQ)	Georgia (WISG, 2012) N=150 (LGB)
Name Calling		38.64%		
Insults	35%	39%		73.33%
Verbal harassment			31%^ 25.8#	49.33%
Harassment		22%		
Mental violence				89.33%
Threat of violence		20%	9.9%#	
Physical violence (unspecified)		15%	8.57%* 3.4%^ 4.2%#	32%
Wounded or assaulted with weapon	2%	.45%		4.0%
Property damaged	4%	11%		4.0%
Objects thrown		8.18%		
Spat at		10.90%		
Punched, hit or kicked	11%	14.55%		
Excluded or ignored		20%		
Sexual assault/violence	3%		0.4%^	
Sexually persecuted		15.0%		
Sexual harassment		22.27%		4.6%
Raped	2%	4.55%		4.0%
Beaten or assaulted by police		13.64%		
Assaulted by police				
Harassed by police		13.64%		
Chased or followed				
Indirect discrimination			24.9%^ 23.0%#	
Discrimination				
Psychological maltreatment			18.2%* 12.4%^	
Maltreatment			12.4% * 10.6% **	
Blackmail	7%		2.6% * 4.2% **	33.33%
Fired/forced to resign		12%	1.1% *** 1.9% **	
Refused work		12%		

Note:
These surveys are presented for illustrative purposes only. The data are not comparable across countries due to differences in methodology, definition of terms, data collection, and analysis.
* Based on sex/gender
** Based on sexual orientation
*** Based on sexual identity, gender identity and/or gender expression

APPENDIX 4: ANECDOTAL INFORMATION ON HUMAN RIGHTS VIOLATIONS IN THE E&E REGION

4A. VIOLATIONS OF FUNDAMENTAL FREEDOMS

ALBANIA

- LGBT who were surveyed revealed that they greatly mistrust the police–they are often kept in jail for many hours without knowing the cause of the arrest, humiliated and are subjected to unjustified police violence (COWI & DIHR, 2010a).

- In March 2010, a participant on the Albanian live television show Big Brother openly revealed his sexual orientation, sparking protests in his hometown. Threats of violence forced his family to flee the town, but police did not stop the unauthorized protests or address hate speech posted on Internet websites (ILGA-Europe, 2011d).

- Police investigating a theft in a park were interviewing people and "amongst the people they were interviewing for the case was also a young man, who is friends with the transgender group, which lives by this park. When the police tried to detain the young man, they faced resistance by one of the transgender people called Paloma" (ILGA-Europe, 2011e). Six police officers beat her, took her into custody, and continued to perpetrate physical violence against her. "To avoid any bruises on the head and face, she was forced to wear a helmet, while kicking and punching continued all over her body…The police took Paloma to Mother Teresa National Hospital (QSUT), where she received immediate aid and was then taken back to the police headquarters of Tirana" (ILGA-Europe, 2011e).

- In Tirana in 2012, an otherwise successful set of events was disturbed by youths throwing small explosives at activists participating in a bicycle "Ride Against Homophobia" through the city center (IDAHO, 2012). The 2013 ride occurred without incident, although participants who went to a bar to celebrate afterwards were targeted by young men who threw tear gas at them (Historia IME, 2013b).

ARMENIA

- A bar, DIY, known to be frequented by both LGBT and straight people was targeted with a homemade bomb in early May, 2012. Bail of approximately US$2,500 was supplied for the bombers by two members of parliament (ARF party) (Armenian Weekly, 2012).

- "The authorities' response to the discrimination and violence perpetrated against gay, lesbian, bisexual, transgender and intersex (LGBTI) people is often slow and inadequate. They frequently condone such attacks, blaming the violence on the expression of "traditional values" rather than issuing strong and unequivocal condemnation" (Amnesty International, 2013).

- "A Diversity March in Yerevan, co-sponsored by PINK and the Women's Resource Centre to mark the UN World Day for Dialogue and Development, was disrupted on 21 March 2012. About 100 counter-demonstrators, carrying placards with slogans like "Send Gays to Baku" and "Armenia without Gays" and shouting abuse and threats. They attacked and injured marchers before the police eventually intervened" (Amnesty International, 2013).

AZERBAIJAN

- In 2005, two lesbians were fired from jobs because of their sexual orientation (G&D et al, 2009).

- In 2007, doctors refused to treat two transsexuals after a car accident (van der Veur, 2007).

- There are two cases of police blackmail or revealing SO of victim to family and employer recorded to the ICCPR in 2008 (G&D et al, 2009).

- In May 2007 in Azerbaijan, 27 transgender persons and gay men were arrested and subjected to severe police violence while in custody. They were also forced to take HIV tests (G&D et al., 2009). In 2011, a local NGO reported "numerous incidents of police brutality against individuals based on sexual orientation…[and] 80 police raids directed at the lesbian, gay, bisexual and transgender (LGBT) community during the year (U.S State Department, 2012).

BELARUS

- Gatherings of LGBT people have been banned in Minsk and elsewhere (ARC, 2010c).

- The attempt to register the organization Gay Belarus resulted in harassment of the LGBT community which included the raid of a gay nightclub and NGO leaders being brought in by the police for questioning. During the night club raid, police filmed participants and made them state their names, place of work, and sexual orientation (Karmanau, 2013).

- The head of Gay Belarus was denied exit from Belarus to travel to the U.S. for training and border guards seized his passport (Karmanau, 2013).

BOSNIA AND HERZEGOVINA

- A cultural event, the Queer Sarajevo Festival, one of the first public events held for LGBT people in Bosnia and Herzegovina, was attacked by demonstrators and Wahhabist religious extremists in 2008. Six people were hospitalized as a result and there were also attacks on the office of the organizers, death threats to the organizers of the festival, and a lack of police protection. Authorities did not address homophobic rhetoric that was broadcast and posted online (Ferrara, 2008; Organization Q, 2008; COWI & DIHR, 2010d).

GEORGIA

- Police raid on offices of Inclusive Foundation 2009—the case is due before the European Court of Human Rights for breaches of Article 3 (inhuman and degrading treatment), Article 8 (interference in private lives), and Article 14, protocol 12, discrimination based on SO. The lack of effective remedies and absence of investigation into the incident also breaches Article 13 of the Convention (ILGA-Europe, 2011c).

- LBT women experience forced marriage and "corrective" rape, as well as cases of physical, sexual and psychological abuse (Natsvlishvili & Aghdgomelashvili, 2012).

- Sex workers (including LGBT) are often victims of police violence (Natsvlishvili & Aghdgomelashvili, 2012).

- The 2007 Council of Europe event "All Different, All Equal," had to be cancelled because it was perceived to be a 'gay parade' by the Orthodox Church who arranged rallies against it and the Patriarch warned authorities of violence if it went ahead (Natsvlishvili & Aghdgomelashvili, 2012).

- In 2009, 2010 (in Batumi) and in May 2012 (Tblisi), demonstrations with Church representatives took place, resulting in violence and intense public negative response (Natsvlishvili & Aghdgomelashvili, 2012; Global voices, 2012).

- The Inclusive Foundation filed a suit with the European Court of Human Rights alleging abuse of power by the police and improper search of their premises in 2009. At the time it was the only formal LGBT NGO in the country (ILGA-Europe, 2011c).

KOSOVO

- In 2007, the director of LGBT organization QESH received repeated death threats – police offered no protection (and he subsequently emigrated). The following year, a friend of his had his throat cut in a bar (not fatal).

- In 2008, a gay man was murdered in a Pristina park, but police refused to see it as a homophobic crime (Immigration and Refugee Board of Canada, 2011).

- There are reports that police officers themselves are often the perpetrators of violence against LGBT people (Immigration and Refugee Board of Canada, 2011).

- The office of the organization Libertas was attacked and a staff member was beaten after leaving the premises (Savic, 2013).

- In 2012, an attempt was made to prevent a launch party for an edition of the magazine *Kosovo 2.0* that examined heterosexual and homosexual sexuality in the Western Balkans. A group of Muslim men attacked the center where the publication launch was scheduled, destroyed equipment, and physically attacked a magazine staffer. Damage was severe, but the four police assigned as guards were able to disperse the men, and the event went on as scheduled with 200 people attending. However, an after-party was cancelled because a group of men returned. Police evacuated the people remaining at the venue (Domi, 2012; Shabani, 2013).

REPUBLIC OF MACEDONIA

- After a pharmacist in Kumanovo was murdered in 2005, police found up that he was homosexual and rounded up all known and suspected gay men for questioning, and in the process many were humiliated and outed to their families and employers (MASSO et al., 2009).

- Two men, discovered by police while having sex in a car, were harassed and forced to have sex. Then, one of them was raped by a police officer (COWI & DIHR, 2010f).

- A license to hold the closing part for the Queer Square festival (Love is Love) in a main square in Skopje was denied on the basis that a statue of Mother Theresa stood on the square and that the LGBT event was morally inappropriate. On the same day another NGO used the same square for an event related to the fight against cancer (MASSO et al., 2009).

- "According to the representative of Ombudsman office, the LGBT population, especially transgender persons, are targets of the special police forces Alpha - a special unit formed to combat street crime" (COWI & DIHR, 2010f).

- A gay police officer on a date was attacked and forced to have oral sex while being filmed. He was suspended from the force, but was later able to return to his job (COWI & DIHR, 2010f).

- "In October [2013], the Macedonian Helsinki Committee opened an LGBTI Support Centre in Skopje with the aim of providing space for LGBTI groups to self-organise and provide support. A day after the opening of the Centre (and following the above mentioned media portrayal of the issue), three masked assailants stoned the Centre and broke the glass at the entrance. The Helsinki Committee reported the attack to the police and the case is under investigation" (ILGA-Europe, 2013a).

- "In October [2013], Spiro Ristovski, the Minister of Labour and Social Policy, reiterated his claims that 'homosexuals cannot raise healthy children' on national TV station SITEL. The journalists of the station presented homosexuality as a threat to the nation and to civilisation, drawing parallels between homosexuality and paedophilia, incest and zoophilia" (ILGA-Europe, 2013a).

- The European Court of Human Rights found violations to freedom of assembly (Article 11), the right to effective legal remedy (Article 13) and the ban on discrimination (Article 14) when hearing the case GenderDoc-M vs Moldova regarding the banned 2005 Chisinau Pride march (GenderDoc-M, 2012b).

- "On 19 and 20 February 2007, police officers demanded identification from young men in a park known to be a popular cruising ground for members of the gay community. When these young men were unable to present their identification, they were taken to the police station, where they were searched and interrogated about their sexual orientation. The police also confiscated any money they had, and some of the men were threatened with physical harm. A complaint filed by GenderDoc-M with the Police Commissariat of Chişinău municipality did lead to punishment for those involved" (COWI & DIHR, 2010g).

- Police are recorded as using deeply offensive language towards LGBT people and blackmailing LGBT people by threatening to out them to family or employers (COWI & DIHR, 2010g).

- Attempts to hold the Pride event Rainbow over the Dniester in 2008 were met with violence when protestors surrounded the bus transporting participants to the parade (Wockner, 2008). Protestors only allowed the bus to move on when all LGBT symbols, such as placards and rainbow flags, were handed over to them. The police did not intervene, saying they did not want to be seen as "gay friendly" (COWI & DIHR, 2010g). The protestors followed the bus to the offices of the NGO GenderDoc-M and insisted that staff of the NGO came out. The event was banned in 2010. A recent report indicates that a Pride march was allowed and protected by police in 2013. Eight individuals participated in the march with the protection of 15–20 police officers (Sindelar, 2013).

- Legislators passed laws banning "homosexual propaganda" in the Moldovan cities of Bălţi,[54] "Cahul, Ceadîr Lunga, Drochia, Rîşcani, Glodeni and Soroca, the districts of Anenii Noi Făleşti and Basarabeasca and the villages of Hiliuţi (Făleşti district), Chetriş (Făleşti district), Bocani and Pîrliţa" (Venice Commission, 2013). In 2013, the decision was annulled in Bălţi, and Făleşti district while Rîşcani, Glodeni, Bocani and Pîrliţ withdrew their decisions.

- In 2011, for the first time a permit was granted for a LGBT public demonstration, but violence forced the event to be cancelled (Intergroup on LGBT rights, 2012).

- The organizer of a planned May 2011 Pride received death threats (ILGA-Europe, 2011d).

- "There is anecdotal evidence of hate crimes against LGBT persons in Podgorica, and that victims of hate crime do not report the incidents to the police. There are also accounts of police abuse or neglect" (COWI & DIHR, 2010h).

- On January 15, 2011 in an interview with the daily newspaper Vijesti, Minster Dinoša denied the existence of discrimination against LGBT people in Montenegro: "Nobody complained to us regarding any form of discrimination in this issue." In a later interview the minister stated he had no intention of challenging the "moral code of the majority" and revealed that his religious beliefs stand above his duties as Minister for Human and Minority Rights (ILGA-Europe 2011d).

- In 2013, Police clashed with anti-gay protesters as they attacked the first gay pride parade to be held in Montenegro. "Around 200 demonstrators hurled stones, bottles and torches at policemen in the coastal town of Budva who were keeping them separate from around 40 marchers wearing shirts bearing the colors of the rainbow, the symbol of the gay rights movement. Protesters chanted "'Kill the gays' and

---

54. Reports indicate that the law was overturned by the Balti Court of Appeals in February 2013 as unconstitutional and violating human rights (RFE/RL's Moldovan Service, 2013.

carried banners that read 'Only healthy Montenegro'" (Zuvela, 2013).

- The first openly gay man in Montenegro was the target of unrelenting death threats (including a fake death notice posted in Budva) before the 2013 Pride event (Feder, 2013).

- Violent clashes occurred during the first Pride parade held in the capital of Montenegro. "Masked anti-gay protesters attacked police cordons and threw stones as they tried to break through and reach the parade, but officers in full riot gear held them back by firing tear gas. Twenty policemen were injured, one of them seriously. Among the 60 people detained, a third of them were under 18, police said" (Milosevic, 2013).

- Protestors were arrested with weapons including Molotov cocktails, metal bars, bricks, and smoke bombs (Ekipa CdM-a, 2013).

RUSSIA

- There have been numerous documented attacks on LGBT people and police are highly mistrusted and implicated in violence against LGBT people. Hate speech is also prevalent; for example, on a radio show in 2008, billionaire Roman Sterligiov said on the air, "Let it be their blood on their heads' and when asked if this means to kill them, he answered, "Yes, for sure" (Kochetkov & Kirichenko, 2008).

- Lesbian activist Irina Fedotova was arrested in March 2009 for holding two posters near a secondary school building that said, "Homosexuality is normal," and "I am proud of my homosexuality." In 2012 the UN Human Rights Committee ruled that her rights to freedom of expression and freedom from discrimination had been violated (UN Human Rights Committee, 2012).

- Organizers of the Side by Side LGBT International Film Festival reported in 2008 and 2010 that they were impeded in their efforts to obtain the required licenses and building repairs, and that there appeared to be purposeful electricity black-outs. Threats against the organizers and participants as well as hate speech were neither stopped nor investigated by police (Russian LGBT Network, 2011). In 2012, the festival was targeted and harassed by small groups of young men (Russian LGBT Network, 2013).

- A Russian court heard the first case under a new St. Petersburg anti-homosexual propaganda law in late April 2012. A person who made the point of saying he was heterosexual had been arrested for carrying a placard decrying the new law (Pink News, 2012b). This was followed by the arrest of 17 people who refused to hand over to the police the rainbow flags they were carrying while participating in the 2012 May Day march in St. Petersburg (Elder, 2012).

- Extreme violence at unsanctioned Pride parades continues unabated in 2013. The attempt to hold a Pride parade in St. Petersburg was met with extreme violence and arrests of LGBT participants (Roller, 2013; Stopera, 2013).

- Videos went viral of abuse of gay men and teenagers by those who had lured them via YouTube and Russian social media sites. Videos are posted online and shared (Broderick, 2013).

- In 2001, LGBT participants were brutally attacked by hordes of neo-nationalist, neo-Nazi and fascist hooligans, and were not protected by the police. Subsequent applications for Pride events in Serbia were denied by the authorities who said they would not guarantee the safety of participants. In 2004 and 2009, Pride events were organized but abandoned due to safety concerns again because the state could not guarantee safety. By 2009 the controversy (amidst massive amounts of hate speech) over Pride went on for months in the media, with the presence of much homophobic graffiti in various cities in Serbia (not removed by authorities). Some Pride organizers felt forced to leave Serbia due to personal threats (COWI & DIHR, 2010j).

- The NGO Gay-Straight Alliance produced a sexual orientation and gender identity-focused hate crime map of 46 incidents that occurred between 2000 and 2009. GSA estimates that the map includes one percent of the actual total, illustrating how victims are afraid of exposure and further discrimination as a result of reporting hate crimes to authorities (GSA, 2010).

- "Some of the messages that appeared on the website of the organization Obraz, sent to the participants of the Gay Pride 2009, include: 'faggots, paedophiles, sodomist, transsexuals, bisexuals, and others will not be tolerated and there will be no mercy, neither from people or God for them. All of you will be strictly punished and eradicated!!!...,' 'the Gay Pride is obvious provocation and they are sticking fingers in our eyes as well in the eyes of the Serbian people. That will not be unpunished. We are waiting for you at the Gay Pride!!!'" (COWI & DIHR, 2010j).

- Many violent incidents have been reported by the Gay Straight Alliance, including being chased, cursed at with anti-LGBT slurs, spat on, punched, kicked, and attacked with knives (GSA, 2011; GSA 2012). These incidents can occur anywhere at any time.

- Human Rights Watch (2013) reported rapes perpetrated with the goal of "curing" lesbians.

- A baseline study carried out for the Young Men's Initative in Belgrade found that out of 620 young men aged 15-19, in the three months before taking the survey, 21 percent had verbally attacked someone they thought was gay, and 13 percent had physically assaulted that person (Care & ICRW, 2010).

- An alleged kidnapping occurred by a LGBT person's family in 2013 with the goal of doing a religious ritual to make him heterosexual (GSA, 2013).

- "There was this lesbian girl who was raped by her sister's husband. She doesn't want to go to police because of the family issues and because of the mistrust for the police. We were also in contact with two girls, who were beaten up in a café. They are afraid to tell anyone at all. There was also a boy, who was raped by eight men. He didn't go to the police either. People do not come out" (COWI & DIHR, 2011k).

- The 2012 Pride in Ukraine was cancelled because "police claimed they could not protect participants from potential violence from neo-Nazi and nationalist groups planning a protest at the same time and location" (Human Rights Watch, 2013).

- In 2010–2011, there were 83 documented violations of LGBT peoples' rights in Ukraine, including hate speech, assault, battery, and rape. One victim reported graffiti on the entrance to his apartment that said "Kill the gays who live here!" He was later beaten up by neighbors (Zinchenkov, et al., 2011).

- It is alleged that police in Ukraine collected personal data on gay men and lesbians in 2010–2011, as well as sought out and intimidated gay men with a goal of collecting personal information of other LGBT people (U.S. Department of State, 2011; U.S. Department of State, 2012).

- Many cases of physical violence have been reported in Ukraine. Beatings have included multiple public attacks on Pride Parade organizers. LGBT people have been attacked on the street, at demonstrations, in the homes of their families, and in the hallways of their apartment buildings. Injuries have ranged from bruises and contusions to tooth loss, a broken nose, a broken jaw, and head injuries (Nash Mir, 2013; LGBT Human Rights Nash Mir Center, 2013a; Human Rights Watch, 2013).

- Pride organizers have been physically attacked directly after press conferences and on the street (Stern, 2012).

- "Hate-motivated actions most often were addressed in connection with the illegal activities of 'Okkupay-pedofilyay' groups. Under the guise of being minors, they meet (entrap) gay men online, and during the personal meeting phase they surround the victim, force him (through fear of violence and sometimes by actual violence) into self-incrimination, and then spread the video of the 'confession' out upon the social networks (LGBT Human Rights Nash Mir Center, 2013a).

- "The second largest group of complaints is issues related to illegal actions of the police through the Internet. In practice, provoking crime has become a popular way to improve the figures of activity for the Ukrainian police. To do this (to bring about entrapment), police officers register at one of the online dating websites for gay men and ask one of its customers to disclose his intimate photos. The act of opening photos, then, entails a criminal charge of pornography distribution, or exacts a bribe for silence. Thus over the last 2-3 years dozens of gay men were prosecuted or forced to pay large bribes to the police for silence" (LGBT Human Rights Nash Mir Center, 2013a).

4B. SOCIO-ECONOMIC HUMAN RIGHTS VIOLATIONS

For all countries:

- *Housing*: Partners must act as friends in order to not experience discrimination when renting apartments together.

- *Asylum*: No data unless otherwise noted.

- *Social security*: No data on discrimination in this area, but same-sex couples are not entitled to insurance or family related social benefits available to opposite-sex partners.

- *Partnership*: Same-sex couples do not have cohabitation, civil partnership or same-sex marriage rights.

ALBANIA

Education: Schoolbooks refer to homosexuality as a disorder requiring treatment. There was a report of a gay teenage boy being refused access to education (ILGA-Europe, 2011d).

Employment: There are few data available, but the general attitude is 'don't ask, don't tell.' There is some evidence that persons not conforming to gender norms are prone to workplace discrimination (GISH, 2006). Many transgender people participate in sex work and experience violence and abuse (Pink Embassy, 2011).

Health: Two transgender women sex workers were initially refused hospital treatment after being stabbed and then were treated in a degrading manner by health staff (COWI & DIHR, 2010a). In 2010, there was a case of a hospital guard asking a doctor whether should he allow "a pederast in" (i.e., a transgender person), to which doctor allegedly replied, "One pederast less, let him die." Treatment was provided after a 45-minute delay (ILGA-Europe, 2011d).

Housing: Young LGBT people have been forced to leave home by their families (COWI & DIHR, 2010a).

Asylum: "There have been several cases of LGBT persons from Albania having applied, and been granted, asylum in other countries" (COWI & DIHR, 2010a).

ARMENIA

Education: Public schools are heavily influenced by the outlook of the Armenian Apostolic Church, which rejects homosexuality and presents a traditionalist approach to gender expression. No support for LGBT students or teachers by school authorities exists, although there are reports of name-calling, bullying and violence.

Employment: There are reports of employers refusing to hire anyone who is open about being LGBT (COWI & DIHR, 2010b). The army has been known to out LGBT recruits and allow degrading treatment (Carroll & Quinn, 2009).

Health: Inadequate knowledge and training of medical staff regarding transgender health is common (COWI & DIHR, 2010b). LGBT people report not seeking health care because they fear that providers will not keep their information confidential and the high risk of seeing a non-LGLBT-friendly doctor (Pink Armenia, 2011a).

Housing: A young man in Gyumri was refused housing because of a newspaper interview he did about LGBT people.

Asylum: "In 2007, an Armenian received legal residence status in the USA, one of the reasons was the document from the psychiatric hospital, diagnosing him as a person with a sexual perversion/disorder, homosexuality" (COWI & DIHR, 2010b).

AZERBAIJAN

Education: "According to Gender & Development, the curricula in public schools do not include sexual education or life skills, and LGBT people are not represented in the educational material" (COWI & DIHR, 2010c).

Employment: There is a lack of data available on discrimination against LGBT people in the workplace. However, "LGBT individuals and representatives reported that employers found other reasons to fire them, such as 'under-performance'" instead of their sexual orientation or gender identity.

Health: "The big taboo on sexuality and HIV/AIDS has contributed to a lack of accurate information on the spread of HIV in Azerbaijan" (van der Veur, 2007). In addition, there have been cases "when transgender persons did not receive proper treatment in the health care institutions" (COWI & DIHR, 2010c).

Asylum: "Some gay Azerbaijani men have been granted asylum in Western Europe (Czech Republic and the Netherlands)" (COWI & DIHR, 2010c).

BELARUS

Education: No data.

Employment: Sparse data. The editor of the Gay.by website alleges being fired from the British American Tobacco company (Canning, 2011).

Health: No data.

BOSNIA AND HERZEGOVINA

Education: Survey respondents reported differential treatment by teachers (e.g., lower grades, more discipline) when they knew or suspected a student was LGBT. They reported teachers describing homosexuality as " a disease, unnatural and abnormal" (COWI & DIHR, 2010d). They also reported ridicule and bullying by peers and teachers. Where textbooks mention sexual orientation, it is presented as a disease.

Employment: Respondents to a 2008 survey report discrimination, including verbal harassment and dismissal (Durkovic, 2008).

Health: Ten of 210 people surveyed in 2008 witnessed discrimination against LGBT people in health facilities (Durkovic, 2008). "Personnel and the doctors (psychologists and psychiatrists) are not educated in LGBT issues and about the specific problems of these groups" (COWI & DIHR, 2010d). The Ministry of Health does not cover gender reassignment surgery, pre- or post-operational treatment, or hormonal therapy under the national health insurance (COWI & DIHR, 2010d).

Housing: There are accounts of housing discrimination when private persons rent out their apartments to individuals or NGOs. Organization Q was evicted when it was found to be a LGBT NGO by the landlord (COWI & DIHR, 2010d).

Asylum: One Cameroonian gay man applied for asylum status in Bosnia and Herzegovina in 2009 (COWI & DIHR, 2010d).

GEORGIA

Education: "According to Inclusive Foundation, derogatory terms referring to LGBT persons are frequently used for bullying and this is one of the reasons why practically no pupils or students come out as LGBT" (COWI & DIHR, 2010e). The curriculum in public schools does not include sexual education or life skills, and LGBT identities and practices are not represented in the curricula" (COWI & DIHR, 2010e). Schools and universities, especially those in smaller cities and rural areas, are strongly influenced by the Georgian Orthodox Church and echo its values.

Employment: "There is anecdotal evidence of cases of harassment and of LGBT persons being fired when outed" (COWI & DIHR, 2010e). New data protection legislation (March 2012) allows the sharing of information without consent of the employee, including information on sexual orientation and gender identity, with third parties (Natsvlishvili & Aghdgomelashvili, 2012).

Health: Medical personnel are reported to exhibit homophobic attitudes (Natsvlishvili & Aghdgomelashvili, 2012). Owing to stigmatization of people living with HIV/AIDS, people avoid diagnosis and treatment (Global Rights and Inclusive Foundation, 2012). HIV/AIDS prevention activities are lacking among high risk groups, which include MSM (COWI & DIHR, 2010e). Sex-reassignment surgery is available, but transgender people must go through a year-long process to be allowed to proceed with surgery (COWI & DIHR, 2010e).

Asylum: Several Georgian LGBT persons have claimed asylum abroad, mostly in the U.S. and Western Europe. One gay man who applied for asylum in Norway in 2005 based on his sexual orientation was refused, and on return to Georgia was stabbed to death in the city of Gori (COWI & DIHR, 2010e).

KOSOVO

Education: No data.

Employment: The high national unemployment rate of 45 percent means that many LGBT persons must rely on their families. Lesbians are especially disadvantaged in that regard due to prevailing attitudes about gender roles (Savic, 2013).

Health: No data.

Asylum: One young gay man reportedly received political asylum in the U.S. after being forced out of the family home and beaten by his parents (Bytyçi, 2007).

REPUBLIC OF MACEDONIA

Education: In May 2011, after lobbying by LGBT and allied groups, an order was passed by Ministry of Education to remove the *Pedagogy* text book for secondary education from use because of its homophobic content describing lesbian and gay people as "highly neurotic and psychotic" and participants in "abnormal, not natural and degenerated sexual life [sic]" (ILGA-Europe, 2013a). The textbook was reprinted in 2012 without the discriminatory language.

Employment: There is a recorded case of a policeman who was fired because he engaged in same-sex relations (COWI & DIHR, 2010f).

Health: "Several of the members of the Women's Alliance have been in situations where they could not visit their same-sex partners in hospital, because they were not recognised as next of kin" (COWI & DIHR, 2010f). Medical practitioners have, in at least one instance, attempted to "cure" homosexuality at a parent's request (MASSO, et al., 2008). There is little information available on medical professionals' treatment of LGBT people.

Housing: There is one (and possibly another) documented case of a male couple being evicted because of their sexual orientation (COWI & DIHR, 2010f).

MOLDOVA

Education: Schools are strongly influenced by the Moldovan Orthodox Church--a life skills program funded by UNICEF that included information on "sexual behavior, diversity, tolerance and homosexuality" was removed from the school curriculum as a result of pressure from it and other churches (COWI & DIHR, 2010g). Outdated medical textbooks are used, which means that students are taught that homosexuality is an illness.

Employment: A male-to-female transgender person who was a teacher at a high school began to undergo hormone treatment and began to express a feminine identity. She was forced to quit her job. In 2008, A bisexual female teacher at a university was forced to resign, rather than being fired, after she was seen kissing another woman (COWI & DIHR, 2010g). Transgender people are often forced to work without a contract at low-salaried positions.

Health: LGBT people deeply mistrust health providers. Results of one survey indicate that doctors are perceived as one of the most homophobic groups in Moldova (COWI & DIHR, 2010g). "Transgender individuals seeking information about sex reassignment and other medical procedures are ridiculed by public health officials and are often not given the information they seek" (GenderDoc-M, et al., 2009). According to "GenderDoc-M", it is here that the person finds out about hormone therapy, gets advice on how and where to buy hormones, which doses to take etc., and starts his/her self-medication. Self-medication is very dangerous for the health, as the wrong doses of hormones can lead to serious heart problems, blood pressure issues, etc." (COWI & DIHR, 2010g).

Asylum: "According to 'HomoDiversus Pro,' there have been very few cases of LGBT persons seeking asylum abroad because of persecution on grounds of sexual orientation or gender identity officially" (COWI & DIHR, 2010g).

MONTENEGRO

Education: Little information is available. Juventas reported that there is no mention of LGBT issues or representation of LGBT persons in the curricula, and that there is extensive bullying of pupils not conforming to the traditional notions of gender" (COWI & DIHR, 2010h).

Employment: Little information is available. "A beneficiary of Juventas has reported to have been fired by an employer who stated that 'we do not want a faggot in our store.' However, he did not want to make a case out of it" (COWI & DIHR, 2010h).

Health: A Ministry of Health representative "call[ed] the situation in health care 'a copy of everyday life', and state[d] that the consequences are that LGBT persons are reluctant to seek proper health Care" (COWI & DIHR, 2010h).

Asylum: Little data. The first openly gay man sought asylum in Canada in 2013, largely because no one was convicted after attacking the Pride parade in Budva (Feder, 2013).

RUSSIA

Education: "Young LGBT persons are often subject to bullying and harassment from their classmates and teachers at schools….Teachers, who choose to come out or are assumed to be homosexual, are also subjected to bullying and harassment on the side of their colleagues and students" (COWI & DIHR, 2010i). When writing their dissertations on LGBT-related topics, several graduate students reported obstacles such as not being allowed to defend their dissertation, being asked to change their dissertation topic, and fielding extra-critical questions during their defense.

Employment: "Disclosure of sexual orientation of a person most frequently leads to their dismissal in Russian towns, after which it is practically impossible for the affected people to find a new job in the same town" (COWI & DIHR, 2010i). I "Many transgender persons, who do not have documents matching their gender expression, may be invited to job-interviews on the basis of their professional skills. But as soon as they present their documents, their appointment is cancelled" (COWI & DIHR, 2010i).

Health: Discriminatory attitudes to LGBT in health care settings (e.g., hospitals and clinics) are widespread. One report notes that one person's experience visiting a friend with HIV in hospital and the nurse saying "this is no place for a meeting of faggots" is not uncommon. It is reported that suitable medical services for transgender people do not exist outside of Moscow and St. Petersburg. "Transgender persons report the complete absence of a professional understanding of transgender issues by general practitioners and other medical staff, leading to degrading and partly false treatment" (COWI & DIHR, 2010i).

Housing: Same-sex couples have been refused access to rental housing. There are instances of neighbors causing LGBT people to be forced to leave their apartments because their neighbors find out or suspect their sexual orientation or gender identity (COWI & DIHR, 2010i).

SERBIA

Education: LGBT people or those thought to be LGBT are often bullied and subjected to violence (COWI & DIHR, 2010j). Textbooks still used for sixth year medical students describes homosexuality as deviant and problematic (GSA, 2010).

Employment: Little inforation is available. A former employee of a media outlet brought a suit against the company and claimed that his sexual orientation was the real reason for his dismissal, but the court refused to consider the relevance of sexual orientation. However, he did win the case, which is being appealed by the company (COWI & DIHR, 2010j).

Health: In 2008, the Serbian Medical Society confirmed that homosexuality is not an illness (Milosevic, 2012). However, LGBT people continue to report being subjected to "treatment" for homosexuality by psychologists and psychiatrists (GSA, 2010). The Belgrade Team for Gender Dysphoria of the Belgrade Center for Genital Reconstructive Surgery provides a full suite of services to transgender people.

UKRAINE

Education: Transgender people report bullying by other school children and discrimination on the part of teachers (COWI & DIHR, 2010k). They also report being refused admittance or not receiving diplomas (Ivantchenko, 2010).

Employment: There are examples of people being denied work or losing their jobs because of their sexual orientation. In April 2009 a gay man from the Donetsk region was hospitalised. A nurse passed information about his sexual orientation, and his HIV-positive status, to his employer, who then fired him (COWI & DIHR, 2010k). Transgender people's anecdotes indicate that they experience overt discrimination in the hiring process, harassment in the workplace, and exploitation by employers (Ivantchenko, 2010).

Health: Health professionals have been known to share personal information related to a patient's sexual orientation with their employers and families. Transgender people are treated insensitively by medical professionals (COWI & DIHR, 2010k). In relation to the lack of trust brought on by poor treatment, there is some anecdotal evidence of self-medication under advice found on the internet (Ivantchenko, 2010).

Asylum: There have been some cases of people applying for asylum from Turkmenistan, Azerbaijan, and Congo (the source document does not specify Democratic Republic of Congo or Congo-Brazzaville) who cited SOGI-based persecution in their home countries, but in all cases there were other circumstances that affected their claims (COWI & DIHR, 2010k).

APPENDIX 5: SAMPLE GENERIC QUESTIONS FOR ANALYSIS

The following questions could be asked when thinking about addressing issues important to LGBT people or engaging with LGBT people and NGOs.

Category	Question
LAWS, POLICIES, AND INSTITUTIONAL PRACTICES	• Are LGBT people protected from discrimination by law? In what areas are they protected against discrimination on the basis of their SO or GI (e.g., education, employment, health care)? • Are LGBT people able to sue or seek mediation for mistreatment, dismissal from employment, or issues with the education system that seems to be related to their SOGI? • Are there laws restricting freedom of speech (e.g., homosexual propaganda laws)? • Is it customary for LGBT events (and people) or NGO offices to be attacked? • Do police protect LGBT people and their property?
ROLES, RESPONSIBILITIES AND TIME USE	• What are the expected roles of lesbians, gay men, bisexual men and women and transgender people in advocacy and the NGO community? • Are LGBT and other NGOs generally willing to work together although they have different interests? • To whom do LGBT activists and NGOS reach out for collaboration? • Around which issues do LGBT NGOs and activists mobilize? • Do gay men, lesbians, and bisexual men and women conform to gender roles? Do MtF and FtM conform to traditional gender roles for their gender identity? • How do LGBT NGOs and activists cooperate with allies and what role do they take? • Are there issues of concern to particular segments of the LGBT population or age groups?
ACCESS TO/CONTROL OVER ASSETS AND RESOURCES	• Do all of the LGBT NGOs have access to the financial resources to mobilize on their issues? If not which do not? • In comparison with the opposition, are LGBT groups sufficiently funded? • Which LGBT NGOs do individuals seek out in order to access services and other benefits? • How does access to safe meeting spaces and online facilities vary across the community?
PATTERNS OF POWER AND DECISION-MAKING	• Which government officials and civil society actors do LGBT organizations influence and at what level (local, national, regional)? • Is there a dialogue between government and civil society on LGBT issues? Who is involved?
CULTURAL PATTERNS	• Who are NGO leaders and activists? Are lesbians, gay men, bisexual men or women, transsexual or transgender people any more or less involved? • How are youth engaged in decision making (age 15-24) in LGBT NGOs, coalitions, and informal groupings? • How free are LGBT people to live openly? • Would participation in a project put LGBT people at risk for being followed, harassed, or attacked?

APPENDIX 6: NATIONAL HUMAN RIGHTS INSTITUTIONS (NHRIS)

Country	Ombudsman Offices for Human Rights	SOGI Inclusive?	Status *	Website
Albania	The People's Advocate	Y	A	http://www.avokatipopullit.gov.al/
Armenia	Human Rights Defender	Y	A	http://www.ombuds.am/
Azerbaijan	Commissioner for Human Rights (Ombudsman)	N	A	http://www.ombudsman.gov.az/view.php?lang=az&menu=0
Belarus	None	N	N/A	
Bosnia and Herzegovina	The Human Rights Ombudsman of Bosnia and Herzegovina	Y	A	http://www.ombudsmen.gov.ba/Jezik.aspx
Georgia	Public Defender	Y	A	http://www.ombudsman.ge/
Kosovo	Republic of Kosovo Ombudsperson	Y: SO N: GI	N/A	http://www.ombudspersonkosovo.org/
Republic of Macedonia	Ombudsman	Y	N/A	http://www.ombudsman.mk/
Moldova	Human Rights Center of Moldova	Y	B	http://www.ombudsman.md/ro
Montenegro	Ombudsman—Protector of Human Rights and Freedoms	Y	N/A	http://www.ombudsman.co.me/
Russia	The Russian Federation's Commissioner for Human Rights	Y	A	http://ombudsmanrf.org/
Serbia	The Protector of Citizens of the Republic of Serbia	Y	A	http://www.zastitnik.rs/
Ukraine	Commissioner for Human Rights	Unclear given recent statements.**	A	http://www.ombudsman.gov.ua/

Notes:

* Status: International Coordinating Committee rates institutions by compliance with the Paris Principles, which "define the minimum conditions that an NHRI must meet if it is to be considered legitimate" (ICC, 2012, OCHCR, 2010). Ratings are:

    A.   Compliant
    B.   Not fully compliant
    C.   Non-compliant

** See Ukrainian Parliament Commissioner for Human Rights, 2013.

APPENDIX 7: LGBT NGOS AND ALLIES IN THE E&E REGION

COUNTRY	LGBT NGOS	ALLIES
Albania	Pink Embassy www.pinkembassy.al/en/lgbt-albania	
Albania	Alliance Against Discrimination of LGBT Persons (Aleanca) http://www.aleancalgbt.org/	
Armenia	Public Information and Need of Knowledge (PINK) Armenia http://www.pinkarmenia.org/en/	Helsinki Association http://hahr.am
Armenia	We for Civil Equality (WFCE) http://www.wfce.am	
Azerbaijan	Gender & Development Social Union	Clean World Aid to Women Social Union http://www.aidsactioneurope.org/members/clean-world-aid-women-social-union
Belarus	Gay Alliance Belarus www.gayby.net	Belarus Free Theatre http://dramaturg.org/
Belarus	GayBelarus Human Rights Project http://gaybelarus.by/	Human Rights Center Viasna http://spring96.org/
Belarus		Meeting http://vstrecha.by/
Belarus		Next Stop New Life https://www.facebook.com/Next.Stop.New.Life
Belarus		RHPA Belarusian Helsinki Committee http://belhelcom.org/
Belarus		Step to Equality http://gender.do.am/
Belarus		Student Parliament http://studrada.org/
Belarus		Youth Social Democrats - Maladaya Hramada www.msd-mh.info
Bosnia and Herzegovina	Organization Q http://www.queer.ba/?q=en/content/organization-q	Sarajevo Open Centre http://soc.ba/
Bosnia and Herzegovina		Human Rights House Sarajevo http://humanrightshouse.org/Members/Bosnia_and_Herzegovina/index.html
Georgia	LGBT Georgia http://www.lgbt.ge	Tanadgoma (HIV) http://new.tanadgomaweb.ge/
Georgia		Women's Initiatives Supporting Group http://women.ge/en (runs the site Lesbi.org.ge)
Georgia		Georgian Young Lawyers Association www.gyla.ge
Kosovo	Center for Social Group Development (CSGD)	
Kosovo	Libertas http://libertas-kos.org/	
Kosovo	Elysium https://www.facebook.com/pages/Elysium-Kosova/335464313143771	
Republic of Macedonia	Equality for Gays and Lesbians (EGAL) http://www.egal.org.mk/en/default.htm	Helsinki Association for Human Rights http://www.hahr.am/index.php/en/

COUNTRY	LGBT NGOS	ALLIES
Republic of Macedonia	LGBT United Macedonia https://www.facebook.com/lgbtunitedmacedonia	
Republic of Macedonia	LGBTI Support Center http://www.lgbti.mk/	Coalition for Protection and Promotion of Sexual and Health Rights of Marginalized Communities http://coalition.org.mk/za-nas/?lang=en
Republic of Macedonia	Women's Alliance http://www.womensalliance.mk/	
Moldova	GenderDoc-M http://www.lgbt.md/eng/	CreDO Resource Center for Human Rights NGOs http://www.credo.md/?&lang=en
Moldova	HomoDiversus Pro https://www.facebook.com/pages/Homo-Diversus/148930268550858	
Montenegro	LGBT Forum Progress http://lgbtprogres.me/	Juventas http://www.juventas.co.me/
Montenegro	Queer Montenegro https://www.facebook.com/pages/Queer-Montenegro/212933025526374	Centre for Antidiscrimination Equista
Russia	Article 282, Moscow see http://www.gayrussia.eu/	
Russia	Coming Out, St. Petersburg http://www.comingoutspb.ru/en/en-home	
Russia	Equality, St Petersburg http://www.spb-pride.ru/	
Russia	FtM Phoenix, Moscow (Trans) http://aronbelkin.narod.ru/FtM_Phoenix.html	
Russia	Lesbiru http://lesbiru.com/	
Russia	LGBT Cooperation ("LGBT Sodejstvije") contact through http://www.lgbtnet.ru/eng/	
Russia	LGBT Human Rights Project "GayRussia," Moscow http://www.gayrussia.eu/	
Russia	Marriage Equality Russia, Moscow http://www.marriageequality.ru/en/	
Russia	Pulsar http://www.pulsarrussia.ru/pulsar	
Russia	Rainbow Association, Moscow contact via http://www.lgbtnet.ru/eng/	
Russia	Rainbow House Tyumen see http://www.lgbtnet.ru/eng/	
Russia	Russian LGBT Network, St Petersburg http://www.lgbtnet.ru/eng/	
Russia	Side by Side, St. Petersburg http://www.bok-o-bok.ru/default.asp?lan=1	
Russia	Together http://www.gay.ru/together/	
Russia	Wings (Krilija), St Petersburg http://www.krilija.sp.ru/en/index.html	
Serbia	Center for Queer Studies http://www.cks.org.rs/	ArtQ (ally) http://arteq.org.rs
Serbia	Labrys http://labris.org.rs/	Lawyers committee For Human Rights http://www.yucom.org.rs/rest.php?idSek=16&idSubSek=56&tip=vestgalerija&status=prvi

COUNTRY	LGBT NGOS	ALLIES
Serbia	Gayten-LGBT www.transserbia.org/ http://www.gay-serbia.com/gayten_lgbt/	Helsinki Committee for Human Rights in Serbia (also active in Kosovo) http://www.helsinki.org.rs/index.html
Serbia	Gay Straight Alliance www.gsa.org.rs/	LGBT Parents http://lgbtroditelji.110mb.com/
Serbia	MaYa LGBT Cultural Center Vojvodina https://www.facebook.com/MayaLgbtKulturniCentarVojvodine	Regional Center for Minorities http://minoritycentre.org/
Serbia	Okvir Okvir.org	Safe Pulse of Youth http://www.spy.org.rs/
Serbia	Queeria http://www.eng.queerbeograd.org/	
Serbia	Support Group for LGBTQ https://www.facebook.com/LGBpodrska	
Ukraine	Agora http://agora0629.org.ua	All-Ukrainian Charitable Organization Time Life Plus http://hivtri.org.ua/partners/lifetimeplus
Ukraine	Association Queer-Credo http://queercredo.org/	All-Ukrainian Coalition of HIV-Service Organizations http://en.hiv.org.ua/home
Ukraine	Donbass-social projects http://donbas-socproject.blogspot.com/	International HIV/AIDS Alliance in Ukraine http://www.aidsalliance.org.ua/cgi-bin/index.cgi?url=/en/news/index.htm
Ukraine	Donetsk Center for LGBT Christians http://lgbtchristians.wix.com/donetsk#!	Kharkiv Human Rights Protection Group http://khpg.org/en/
Ukraine	Fulcrum http://t-o.org.ua/en/	Partner http://mypartner.org.ua/
Ukraine	For Equal Rights, Kherson http://www.zrp-kherson.org.ua/	Road to Life HIV Service Organization http://doroga-zhizni.com/
Ukraine	Gay Alliance Cherkasy http://gayck.at.ua	SOFIR Ukrainina Women's Union http://sphere.in.ua/
Ukraine	Gay Alliance, Ukraine http://ilga.org/directory/en/detail?o_id=6297	Ukrainian Women's Fund http://www.uwf.kiev.ua/en_index.htm
Ukraine	Gay Forum Ukraine http://www.gay-forum.org.ua/	Women's Sports Club «NRG» http://www.nrg.in.ua/o-nas
Ukraine	Insight http://www.insight-ukraine.org.ua/	
Ukraine	LGBT Ukraine http://lgbtua.com/	
Ukraine	LiGA, Nikolaev Association for Gays, Lesbians and Bisexuals http://www.gay.nikolaev.ua/	
Ukraine	New Wave http://novaya-volna.org.ua/	
Ukraine	Our Center, Dnipropetrovsk http://vk.com/club21614878	
Ukraine	Our World (Nash Mir) http://www.gay.org.ua/	
Ukraine	You are not Alone, Zhitomer LGBT Union http://tno.at.ua/	

APPENDIX 8: SHADOW REPORTS SUBMITTED BY OR ON BEHALF OF LGBT

Country	ICCPR	ICESCR	CEDAW	Universal Periodic Review	Europea Commis
Albania				Human Rights Watch, 2009	ILGA-Euro 2011d
Armenia	Pink Armenia, 2011			Canadian HIV/AIDS Legal Network, Eurasian Harm Reduction Network, International Drug Policy Consortium, 2009	
Azerbaijan			Gender & Development, 2009	The Center "Women and Modern World, LGBT Organization Labrys (Kyrgyzstan), and the Sexual Rights Initiative, 2009	
Belarus				LGBT Human Rights Project GayBelarus.By, 2009	
Bosnia and Herzegovina	Global Rights Organization LOGOS, Organization Q, 2007			Organization Q and the Sexual Rights Imitative, 2010 Informal NGO Coalition for UPR (30 NGOs), 2010	ILGA-Euro 2011d
Georgia	Global Rights & Inclusive Foundation, 2007		Natsvlishvili & Aghdgo-melashvili, 2012	ILGA -Europe, COC Netherlands, the Office of Public Defender (Ombudsman) of Georgia, & Inclusive Foundation, 2011	
Kosovo					ILGA-Euro 2011d
Republic of Macedonia	Macedonian Association for Free Sexual Orientation (MASSO), Global Rights, ILGA-Europe , 2008			Informal Coalition Macedonia without discrimination, which includes MASSO, 2011	ILGA-Euro 2011d
Moldova	GenderDoc-M et al, 2009			GenderDoc-M, 2011b	
Montenegro				Sexual Rights Initiative, 2008	ILGA-Euro 2011d
Russia	Global Rights ILGA-Europe, Russian LGBT Network, FtM Phoenix Group, & Russian Transgender Fund, 2009	LGBT Network, 2011	LGBT Network, 2010	Coalition of Russian NGOs (all are not named), 2009 ILGA-Europe, 2012 LGBT Network, 2012	
Serbia	Regional Centre for Minorities Harvard Law School and Heartland Alliance for Human Needs and Human Rights, 2010			Front Line, 2008 Society for Threatened Peoples, 2012 Labrys and Gayten-LGBT, 2012c	ILGA-E, 2(
Ukraine			Insight, 2010	All Ukrainian Union The Council of LGBT organizations of Ukraine, 2012 Nash Mir Gay and Lesbian Center, 2007	

Note: All of these reports were drafted based on contributions from local and national **LGBT** NGOs and are included in the referenc

REFERENCES

3rd View. (2010, June 14). Public Opinion survey on moral and social stance of Azerbaijani youth. Retrieved from http://3view.az/articles/9295/1/

Administration of Saint Petersburg. (2012, march 11). Governor signed the Saint Petersburg law "Amendment ot the law of Saint Petersburg 'On administrative offenses in Saint Petersburg.'" Official ortal Administration of Saint Petersburg. Retrieved from http://old.gov.spb.ru/news8592.html/

AIDSTAR 2. (2010, November). *Men having sex with men in Eastern Europe: Implications of a hidden HIV epidemic.* Washington, D.C.: USAID. Retrieved from http://www.aidstar-two.org/upload/MSM-Regional-Report_Final_November-2-2010.pdf

All-Ukrainian Union The Council of LGBT Organizations of Ukraine. (2012). *The Universal Periodic Review.* Kyiv: Author. Retrieved from http://lib.ohchr.org/HRBodies/UPR/Documents/Session14/UA/CLGBT_UPR_UKR_S14_2012_TheCouncilofLesbianGayBiandTransexual_E.pdf

American Psychiatric Association. (2013). Gender dysphoria. American Psychiatric Publishing. Retrieved from http://www.dsm5.org/Documents/Gender%20Dysphoria%20Fact%20Sheet.pdf

American Psychological Association. (2008). *Report of the APA task force on gender identity and gender variance.* http://www.apa.org/pi/lgbt/resources/policy/gender-identity-report.pdf

American Psychological Association. (2011). *Guidelines for psychological practice with lesbian, gay, and bisexual clients.* Retrieved from http://www.apa.org/pi/lgbt/resources/guidelines.aspx#1

Amnesty International. (n.d.). The "job" of a UN special procedure mandate-holder. Learn about human rights. Retrieved from http://www.amnesty.org/en/united-nations/special-procedures/the-job

Amnesty International. (2013). Armenia: No space for difference. London. Retrieved from http://www.amnesty.org/en/library/asset/EUR54/002/2013/en/6d6a852f-6494-4ef5-bc13-1373f154e0de/eur540022013en.pdf

A'Mula, S. (2009, September 23). The secret life of Kosovo's gay community. *LGBT Asylum News* (original source: Balkan Insight). Retrieved from http://madikazemi.blogspot.com/2009/09/secret-life-of-kosovos-gay-community.html

ARC International. (n.d.). SOGI Statements. Retrieved April 20, 2012, from http://arc-international.net/global-advocacy/sogi-statements

ARC International. (2008a). Summary of Montenegrin SOGI-relevant material submitted to the 3rd Session of the Universal Periodic Review (UPR). Retrieved from http://arc-international.net/global-advocacy/universal-periodic-`review/m/montenegro

ARC International. (2008b). Summary of Serbian SOGI-relevant material submitted to the 3rd Session of the Universal Periodic Review (UPR). Retrieved from http://arc-international.net/global-advocacy/universal-periodic-review/s/serbia

ARC International. (2008c). Summary of Ukrainian SOGI-relevant material submitted to the 2nd Session of the Universal Periodic Review (UPR). Retrieved from http://arc-international.net/global-advocacy/universal-periodic-review/u/ukraine

ARC International (2009a). Summary of Albanian SOGI-relevant material submitted to the 6th Session of the Universal Periodic Review (UPR). Retrieved from http://arc-international.net/global-advocacy/universal-periodic-review/a/albania

ARC International (2009b). Summary of Azeri SOGI-relevant material submitted to the 6th Session of the Universal Periodic Review (UPR). Retrieved from http://arc-international.net/global-advocacy/universal-periodic-review/a/azerbaijan

64

ARC International. (2009c). Summary of Russian SOGI-relevant material submitted to the 4th Session of the Universal Periodic Review (UPR). Retrieved from http://arc-international.net/global-advocacy/universal-periodic-review/o-r/russian-federation

ARC International (2010a). Summary of Armenian SOGI-relevant material submitted to the 6th Session of the Universal Periodic Review (UPR). Retrieved from http://arc-international.net/global-advocacy/universal-periodic-review/a/armenia

ARC International. (2010b). Summary of Belarusian SOGI-relevant material submitted to the 8th Session of the Universal Periodic Review (UPR). Retrieved from http://arc-international.net/global-advocacy/universal-periodic-review/b/belarus

ARC International (2010c). Summary of Bosnian-Herzegovinian SOGI-relevant material submitted to the 7th Session of the Universal Periodic Review (UPR). Retrieved from http://arc-international.net/global-advocacy/universal-periodic-review/b/bosnia-and-herzegovina

ARC International. (2011a). Summary of Georgian SOGI-relevant material submitted to the 10th Session of the Universal Periodic Review (UPR). Retrieved from http://arc-international.net/global-advocacy/universal-periodic-review/g/georgia

ARC International. (2011b). Summary of Moldovan SOGI-relevant material submitted to the 12th Session of the Universal Periodic Review (UPR). Retrieved from http://arc-international.net/global-advocacy/universal-periodic-review/o-r/republic-of-moldova

Armenian Weekly. (2012, May 15). Hate crime targets gay-friendly bar in Yerevan, MPs bail out assailants. Retrieved from http://www.armenianweekly.com/2012/05/15/hate-crime-targets-gay-friendly-bar-in-yerevan-mps-bail-out-assailants/

Asexual Visibility and Education Network. (n.d.). Overview. Retrieved from http://www.asexuality.org/home/overview.html

Assembly of Kosovo. (2001). Law No. 2004/3. The anti-discrimination law. Retrieved from https://www.google.com/url?sa=t&rct=j&q=&esrc=s&source=web&cd=1&ved=0CC8QFjAA&url=http%3A%2F%2Flegislationline.org%2Fdownload%2Faction%2Fdownload%2Fid%2F3507%2Ffile%2FKosovo_Assembly_Anti_Discrimination_Law_2004_en.pdf&ei=hHPIUZn0A4X_4AOUz4HYBw&usg=AFQjCNHTe5BotWdlxu-zT6rVDV9ckXFdxA&sig2=n4U6I28FGvdfec5uAzwisA&bvm=bv.48293060,d.dmg

Assembly of the Republic of Albania. (2010). Law No. 10 221 dated 4.2.2010 on protection from discrimination. Retrieved from http://www.legislationline.org/topics/topic/84/country/47

Associated Press. (2013, July 24). Opponents throw rocks, bottles, clash with police at Montenegrin gay pride event. *Washington Post*. Retrieved from http://www.washingtonpost.com/national/extremists-throw-rocks-bottles-at-montenegrin-gay-activists-at-pride-event/2013/07/24/294173d4-f44c-11e2-81fa-8e83b3864c36_story.html

Association for Health Education and Research. (n.d.). Youth. What We Do. Skopje. Retrieved from http://hera.org.mk/?page_id=592

Astrea Lesbian Foundation for Justice. (2012, November 16). Controversy in Serbia over gender identity law. Latest News. Retrieved from http://www.astraeafoundation.org/news/263/60/Controversy-in-Serbia-over-Gender-Identity-Law

Balkan Insight. (2011, June 14). Opinion poll points to discrimination in Montenegro. Retrieved from http://www.balkaninsight.com/en/article/new-poll-addresses-discrimination-in-montenegro

Balkan Insight. (2012, March 28). Albania minister's anti-gay rant condemned. Retrieved from http://www.balkaninsight.com/en/article/albania-official-anti-gay-comments-condemned

Balzer, C., & Hutta, J.S. (2012). Transrespect versus transphobia worldwide. A comparative review of the human0rights situation of gender-variant/trans people. Transgender Europe & Transrespect versus Transphobia Worldwide. Retrieved from http://www.transrespect-transphobia.org/uploads/downloads/Publications/TvT_research-report.pdf

Barlovac, B. (24 May 2010). Serbia "Becoming sex-change surgery hot spot. Balkan Insight. Retrieved from http://www.balkaninsight.com/en/article/serbia-becoming-sex-change-surgery-hot-spot

BBC News. (2013, May 25). Ukraine stages first gay pride march. News Europe. Retrieved from http://www.bbc.co.uk/news/world-europe-22667015

BBC News. (2012, May 17). Fighting at gay rights march in Tbilisi Georgia. Retrieved from http://www.bbc.co.uk/news/world-europe-18109022

Besic, M. (2011). *Public opinion research on discrimination of minority population and marginalized social groups Montenegro.* Podgorica: Centre for Democracy and Human Rights. Retrieved from http://cedem.me/en/programmes/empirical-research/other-opinion-polls/finish/41-other-opinion-polls/223-public-opinion-research-on-discrimination-of-minority-population-and-marginalized-social-groups-june-2011.html

Bielecki, T. (2013, February 6). Ukraina chce szybkiego podpisania umowy stowarzyszeniowej z UE. *Gazety Wyboxczej.* Retrieved from http://wyborcza.pl/1,76842,13353882,Ukraina_chce_szybkiego_podpisania_umowy_stowarzyszeniowej.html

Bilefsky, D. (2012, July 23). Serbia becomes a hub for sex-change surgery. *The New York Times.* Retrieved from http://www.nytimes.com/2012/07/24/world/europe/serbia-becomes-a-hub-for-sex-change-surgery.html

Bortnik. V.(2011, September 1). *Paper: Basis of claims and background information on LGBT asylum-seekers and refugees from Belarus.* LGBT Asylum News. Retrieved April 23, 2012, from http://madikazemi.blogspot.ie/2011/09/paper-basis-of-claims-and-background.html

Boissevain, J. (8 December 2011). Moldova internet spat sparks free speech debate. Netprophet Weblog. Retrieved from http://netprophet.tol.org/2011/12/08/moldova-internet-spat-sparks-free-speech-debate/

Broderick, R. (2013 July 29). Russians are using social media to lure in and publicly humiliate gay men. Buzzfeed. Retrieved from http://www.buzzfeed.com/ryanhatesthis/russians-are-using-social-media-to-lure-in-and-publicly-humi

Bytyçi, A. (2007). The rights of homosexuals in Kosovo. *Scoop.* Retrieved from http://i-scoop.org/scoop/blog/2007/11/28/the-rights-of-homosexuals-in-kosovo-2/

Canadian HIV/AIDS Legal Network, Eurasian Harm Reduction Network, International Drug Policy Consortium. (2009). Universal Periodic Review Working Group. Review of Republic of Armenia. Retrieved from http://lib.ohchr.org/HRBodies/UPR/Documents/Session8/AM/JS1_UPR_ARM_S08_2010_JointSubmission1.pdf

Canning, P. (2011, October 21). Belarus gay activist says British company fired him because he is gay. *LGBT Asylum News.* Retrieved May 2, 2012, from http://anti-wycliffite.rssing.com/browser.php?indx=1375744&item=1582

Care & ICRW. (2009). Young Men Initiative for Prevention of Gender-Based Violence in Western Balkans baseline research technical brief – country report Bosnia and Herzegovina. Retrieved from http://www.endvawnow.org/uploads/browser/files/CARE_ICRW_BiH_Baseline.pdf

Care & ICRW. (2010). *Young Men Initiative for Prevention of Gender-Based Violence in Western Balkans baseline research technical brief – country report Serbia.* Retrieved from http://www.endvawnow.org/uploads/browser/files/CARE_ICRW_Serbia_Baseline.pdf

Carroll, A. (2010, October). *Make it work: six steps to effective LGBT human rights advocacy.* Brussels: ILGA-Europe. Retrieved from http://ilga-europe.org/home/publications/reports_and_other_materials

Carroll, A., & Quinn, S. (2009). *Forced out: LGBT people in Armenia.* Brussels: International Lesbian and Gay Association – European Region. Retrieved from http://www.ilga-europe.org/home/publications/reports_and_other_materials

Carroll, J B. (1956). Language, thought, and reality: Selected writings of Benjamin Lee Whorf. Boston: M.I.T. Press.

Caucasus Research Resource Centers (CRRC). (2011). Caucasus barometer 2011 for Georgia, Azerbaijan, and Armenia. Online data analysis. Retrieved from http://www.crrc.ge/oda/

CBC News. (2013, August 11). Gay Russian man seeks refugee status in Vancouver. Maxim Zhuravlev says stay in Vancouver homeless shelter safer than life in Russia. *CBC News.* Retrieved from http://www.cbc.ca/news/canada/british-columbia/gay-russian-man-seeks-refugee-status-in-vancouver-1.1365688

The Center "Women and Modern World, LGBT Organization Labrys (Kyrgyzstan), and the Sexual Rights Initiative. (2009). Report on Azerbaijan. Fourth round of the Universal Periodic Review. Retrieved from http://lib.ohchr.org/HRBodies/UPR/Documents/Session4/AZ/WMW_AZE_UPR_S4_2009_WomenandModernWorld_etal_JOINT_upr.pdf

Chechurina. I. (2012, June 26). Samara adopted a law prohibiting propaganda of homosexuality and pedophilia. Russian Gazette. Samara. Retrieved from http://www.rg.ru/2012/06/26/reg-pfo/zakon-anons.html

Clinton, H.R. (2011, December 6). Remarks in Recognition of International Human Rights Day. Geneva, Washington, D.C.: U.S. Department of State. Retrieved from http://lib.ohchr.org/HRBodies/UPR/Documents/Session4/RU/RussianNGOs_RUS_UPR_S4_2009_RussianNGOs_Etal_JOINT.pdfhttp://www.state.gov/secretary/rm/2011/12/178368.htm

Coalition of Russian NGOs. (2008). Materials prepared by Russian NGOs for the Universal Periodic Review of Russia in the United National Human Rights Council. Retrieved from http://www.sova-center.ru/en/xenophobia/conference-papers/2009/02/d15213/

Coalition of Sexual and health Rights of Marginalized Communities. (7 April 2011). Macedonia must protect LGBT people. Retrieved from http://coalition.org.mk/2011/04/makedonija-mora-da-gi-zastiti-lgbt-lug/?lang=en

COC Netherlands. (n.d.). Home page. Retrieved from http://www.coc.nl/dopage.pl?thema=any&pagina=algemeen&algemeen_id=274

Collumbien, M , Busza, J , Cleland, J., & Campbell, O. (2012). *Social science methods for research on sexual and reproductive health.* Geneva: World Health Organization. Retrieved from http://whqlibdoc.who.int/publications/2012/9789241503112_eng.pdf

Commissioner for Human Rights in the Russian Federation. (2009-2012). Official website of the Commissioner for Human Rights in the Russian Federation. Retrieved from http://ombudsmanrf.org/

Council of Europe (CoE). (n.d.a). 47 countries. Homepage. Retrieved February 2012 from http://hub.coe.int/

Council of Europe (CoE). (n.d.b) Activities. Retrieved June 20, 2013 from http://www.coe.int/t/dg4/lgbt/Project/Activities_EN.asp

Council of Europe (CoE). (n.d.c). *Country thematic studies on homophobia, transphobia and discrimination on grounds of sexual orientation and gender identity.* Retrieved March 20, 2012, from http://www.coe.int/t/commissioner/activities/Themes/LGBT/nationalreports_en.asp

Council of Europe (CoE). (n.d.d) Our objectives. Retrieved from http://www.coe.int/aboutCoe/index.asp?page=nosObjectifs&l=en

Council of Europe (CoE). (2000). *Protocol No. 12 to the Convention for the Protection of Human Rights and Fundamental Freedoms (ETS No. 177): Explanatory Report.* Retrieved from http://conventions.coe.int/treaty/en/reports/html/177.htm

Council of Europe (CoE). (2010a). Recommendation CM/Rec(2010)5 of the Committee of Ministers to member states on measures to combat discrimination on grounds of sexual orientation or gender identity. Retrieved from https://wcd.coe.int/ViewDoc.jsp?id=1606669

Council of Europe (CoE). (2010b, June). *Toolkit to Promote and Protect the Enjoyment of all Human Rights by Lesbian, Gay, Bisexual and Transgender (LGBT) People.* Retrieved from http://www.consilium.europa.eu/uedocs/cmsUpload/st11179.en10.pdf

Council of Europe (CoE). (2011a). *Discrimination on grounds of Sexual Orientation and Gender Identity in Europe.* 2nd edition. Strasbourg: Council of Europe Publishing. Retrieved from http://book.coe.int/EN/ficheouvrage.php?PAGEID=36&lang=EN&produit_aliasid=2622

Council of Europe (CoE). (2011b, June). *Council of Europe standards. Combating discrimination on grounds of sexual orientation or gender identity.* Strasbourg: Council of Europe Publishing. Retrieved from http://www.coe.int/t/dghl/standardsetting/hrpolicy/Publications/LGBT_EN.pdf

Council of Europe (CoE). (2011c, May). *Council of Europe convention on preventing and combating violence against women and domestic violence* (CETS 210). Retrieved from http://conventions.coe.int/Treaty/EN/Treaties/Html/210.htm

Council of Europe (CoE). (2012a, April 24). "Fighting discrimination against LGBT is at the heart of our mission," PACE General Rapporteur says. *Parliamentary Assembly of the Council of Europe.* Retrieved from http://assembly.coe.int/ASP/NewsManager/EMB_NewsManagerView.asp?ID=7619&L=2

Council of Europe (CoE). (2012b). LGBT Issues Unit. Combatting discrimination on the grounds of sexual orientation or gender identity. *Parliamentary Assembly of the Council of Europe.* Retrieved from http://www.coe.int/t/dg4/lgbt/Unit/Unit_EN.asp

Council of Europe (CoE) Parliamentary Assembly. (1994). Resolution 1031 on the honouring of commitments entered into by member states when joining the Council of Europe. Retrieved from http://assembly.coe.int/Documents/AdoptedText/TA94/ERES1031.HTM

COWI. The Danish Institute for Human Rights. (2010a). Study on homophobia, transphobia and discrimination on grounds of sexual orientation and gender identity: sociological report: Albania. Council of Europe. Retrieved from http://www.coe.int/t/Commissioner/Source/LGBT/AlbaniaSociological_E.pdf

COWI & The Danish Institute for Human Rights (DIHR). (2010b). Study on homophobia, transphobia and discrimination on grounds of sexual orientation and gender identity: sociological report: Armenia. Council of Europe. Retrieved from http://www.coe.int/t/Commissioner/Source/LGBT/ArmeniaSociological_E.pdf

COWI & The Danish Institute for Human Rights (DIHR). (2010c). Study on homophobia, transphobia and discrimination on grounds of sexual orientation and gender identity: sociological report: Azerbaijan. Council of Europe. Retrieved from http://www.coe.int/t/Commissioner/Source/LGBT/AzerbaijanSociological_E.pdf

COWI & The Danish Institute for Human Rights (DIHR). (2010d). Study on homophobia, transphobia and discrimination on grounds of sexual orientation and gender identity: sociological report Bosnia Herzegovina. Council of Europe. Retrieved from http://www.coe.int/t/Commissioner/Source/LGBT/BosniaHerzegovinaSociological_E.pdf

COWI & The Danish Institute for Human Rights DIHR). (2010e). Study on homophobia, transphobia and discrimination on grounds of sexual orientation and gender identity: sociological report: Georgia. Council of Europe. Retrieved from http://www.coe.int/t/Commissioner/Source/LGBT/GeorgiaSociological_E.pdf

COWI & The Danish Institute for Human Rights (DIHR). (2010f). Study on homophobia, transphobia and discrimination on grounds of sexual orientation and gender identity: sociological report: Macedonia. Council of Europe. Retrieved from http://www.coe.int/t/Commissioner/Source/LGBT/FYROMSociological_E.pdf

COWI & The Danish Institute for Human Rights (DIHR). (2010g). Study on homophobia, transphobia and discrimination on grounds of sexual orientation and gender identity: sociological report: Moldova. Council of Europe. Retrieved from http://www.coe.int/t/Commissioner/Source/LGBT/MoldovaSociological_E.pdf

COWI & The Danish Institute for Human Rights (DIHR). (2010h). Study on homophobia, transphobia and discrimination on grounds of sexual orientation and gender identity: sociological report: Montenegro. Council of Europe. Retrieved from http://www.coe.int/t/Commissioner/Source/LGBT/MontenegroSociological_E.pdf

COWI & The Danish Institute for Human Rights (DIHR). (2010i). Study on homophobia, transphobia and discrimination on grounds of sexual orientation and gender identity: sociological report: Russian Federation. Council of Europe. Retrieved from http://www.coe.int/t/Commissioner/Source/LGBT/RussiaSociological_E.pdf

COWI & The Danish Institute for Human Rights (DIHR). (2010j). Study on homophobia, transphobia and discrimination on grounds of sexual orientation and gender identity: sociological report Serbia. Council of Europe. Retrieved from http://www.coe.int/t/Commissioner/Source/LGBT/SerbiaSociological_E.pdf

COWI & The Danish Institute for Human Rights (DIHR). (2010k). Study on homophobia, transphobia and discrimination on grounds of sexual orientation and gender identity: sociological report: Ukraine. Council of Europe. Retrieved from http://www.coe.int/t/Commissioner/Source/LGBT/UkraineSociological_E.pdf

Cozzarelli, C. (2010, April). *2010 gender assessment for USAID/Serbia*. Washington, D.C.: USAID. Retrieved from http://serbia.usaid.gov/upload/documents/Jrga/USAID%20Serbia%202010%20Gender%20Assessment.pdf

Danchev, D. (04 March 2009). Russian homosexual sites under (commissioned) DDoS attack. Danch Danchev's Blog – Mind Streams of Information Security Knowledge. Retrieved from http://ddanchev.blogspot.com/2009/03/russian-homosexual-sites-under.html

Davis, L. (2008). End of the rainbow: Increasing the sustainability of LGBT organizations through social enterprise. NESst. Retrieved from http://www.nesst.org/galeforce-capital/eotr/

DevTech Systems. Inc. (2010b, August). *Gender assessment USAID/Armenia*. Washington, D.C.: USAID. Retrieved from http://www.devtechsys.com/assets/Uploads/docs/publications/armenia-gender-assessment-2010-08.pdf

Domi., T. (2012, December 15). Update: Organized thugs attack Kosovo 2.0 magazine launch of sexuality edition. *The New Civil Rights Movement*. Retrieved from http://thenewcivilrightsmovement.com/organized-thugs-attack-kosovo-2-0-magazine-launch-sexuality-edition/news/2012/12/15/56422

Duban, E., & Chkheidze, K. (2010a, June). *Gender assessment USAID/Georgia*. Washington, D.C.: USAID & DevTech Systems. Inc.. Retrieved from http://pdf.usaid.gov/pdf_docs/PNADS884.pdf

Duisin, D., Nikolic-Balkoski, N., & Batinic, B. (2009). Sociodemographic profile of transsexual patients. *Psychiatria Danubina, 21 (2), 220-223*. Retrieved from https://www.google.com/url?sa=t&rct=j&q=&esrc=s&source=web&cd=14&cad=rja&ved=0CEIQFjADOAo&url=http%3A%2F%2Fhrcak.srce.hr%2Ffile%2F62545&ei=gGozUtuyE4W24APhooGYCQ&usg=AFQjCNHZmqOHK-94MC9jXFeuDTrCEfcVkQ&sig2=zoVY2Yjx9xkE4BMRNLJm8Q

Durkovic, S. (2008). *The Invisible Q? Human rights issues and concerns of LGBTIQ persons in Bosnia and Herzegovina*. Sarajevo: Organization Q. Retrieved from http://www.queer.ba/files/TheInvisibleQ.pdf

Eguren, E, & Caraj, M. (2010). *Protection manual for LGBTI defenders*. Brussels: Protection International. Retrieved from http://www.protectionline.org/IMG/pdf/LGBTI_PMD_2nd_Ed_English.pdf

Ekipa CdM-a. (2013, October 20). Foto: Završen Montenegro prajd, privedeno 60 osoba, povrijeđeno 20 policajaca. CDM. Podgorica. Retrieved from http://www.cdm.me/drustvo/crna-gora/live-poceo-montenegro-prajd

Euronews. (2012, May 17). Georgia gay pride march ends in fist fight. Retrieved from
http://www.euronews.com/2012/05/17/georgia-gay-pride-march-ends-in-fist-fight/

European Commission (EC). (n.d.)What is EIDHR? Democracy and human rights. Brussels. Retrieved from
http://www.eidhr.eu/whatis-eidhr

European Commission (EC). (2007). Eurobarometer data. Retrieved from
http://ec.europa.eu/public_opinion/archives/ebs/ebs_263_fiche_ro.pdf

European Commission (EC). (2013). Candidate and potential candidate countries. International issues. Retrieved
from http://ec.europa.eu/environment/enlarg/enlargement_en.htm

European Commission (EC) & Council of Europe (COE). (n.d.). Youth policy in Serbia. Youth Partnership.
Retreived from http://youth-partnership-eu.coe.int/youth-partnership/ekcyp/By_country/Serbia.html

European Commission High Representative of the European Union for Foreign Affairs and Security Policy. (2012).
Eastern Partnership roadmap 2012-13: The bilateral dimension. Brussels: European Commission. Retrieved
from http://ec.europa.eu/world/enp/docs/2012_enp_pack/e_pship_bilateral_en.pdf

European Court of Human Rights. (2011). Case of Alekseyev v. Russia. Applications nos. 4916/07, 25924/08 and
14599/09. Judgment. Strasbourg. Retrieved from http://hudoc.echr.coe.int/sites/eng/pages/search.aspx?i=001-
101257

European Court of Human Rights. (2012). About the court. Strasbourg: CoE. Retrieved from
http://www.echr.coe.int/Documents/Court_in_brief_ENG.pdf

European Court of Human Rights. (2013a). Factsheet—Gender identity issues. Strasbourg: CoE. Retrieved from
http://www.echr.coe.int/Documents/FS_Gender_identity_ENG.pdf

European Court of Human Rights. (2013b). Factsheet--Sexual orientation issues. Strasbourg: CoE. Retrieved from
http://echr.coe.int/Documents/FS_Sexual_orientation_ENG.pdf

European Network Against Racism (ENAR). (2011, July). *ENAR factsheet 44: The legal implications of multiple
discrimination.* Retrieved from http://cms.horus.be/files/99935/MediaArchive/publications/FS44%20-
%20The%20legal%20implications%20of%20multiple%20discrimination%20final%20EN.pdf

The European Parliament's Intergroup on LGBT Rights. (2012). Excerpts LGBT rights in the 2012 accession
reports. European Commission. Retrieved from http://www.lgbt-ep.eu/wp-content/uploads/2012/10/DOC-
20121011-EU-accession-progress-reports-LGBT-Intergroup.pdf

European Union. (2010). Partnership and Cooperation *Agreements (PCAs): Russia, Eastern Europe, the* Southern
Caucasus and Central Asia. *Europa. Retrieved from*
http://europa.eu/legislation_summaries/external_relations/relations_with_third_countries/eastern_europe_a
nd_central_asia/r17002_en.htm

Feder, J. (2013, October 21). Montenegro's "First openly gay man," target of death threats, attends Pride march by
Skype. BuzzFeed World. Retrieved from http://www.buzzfeed.com/lesterfeder/montenegros-first-openly-gay-
man-target-of-death-threats-att

Federal Bureau of Investigation. (n.d.) Hate crime—Overview. About us, what we investigate, civil rights, hate
crimes overview. Retrieved from http://www.fbi.gov/about-us/investigate/civilrights/hate_crimes/overview

Ferrara, C. (2008 September 30). Kristalnacht in Sarajevo. Osservatorio Balcani e Caucaso. Retrieved from
http://www.balcanicaucaso.org/eng/Regions-and-countries/Bosnia-and-Herzegovina/Kristalnacht-in-Sarajevo

Freedom House. (2011). Nations in Transit 2011. Retrieved April 20, 2012, from:
http://www.freedomhouse.org/report/nations-transit/nations-transit-2011

Front Line. (2008). [Stakeholder report]. Brussels: Author. Retrieved from
http://lib.ohchr.org/HRBodies/UPR/Documents/Session3/RS/FL_SRB_UPR_S3_2008_FrontLine_uprsubmissio
n.pdf

Gay Alliance Belarus. (2010). *Results of monitoring the situation of homosexuals in the Republic of Belarus in 2009.* Retrieved from http://www.msmgf.org/files/msmgf//Eastern%20Europe%20Central%20Asia/Belarus_LGBT_Report_2009_Gay_Alliance_Belarus.pdf

Gay Straight Alliance (GSA). (2007). *We'll do it fine with a little help from growing group of our friends: report on the LGBT human rights in Serbia in 2007.* Retrieved from http://www.ilga-europe.org/content/download/16760/108431/file/Annual%20Report%20on%20Human%20Rights%20on%20LGBT%20People%20in%20Serbia%20in%202007.doc

Gay Straight Alliance (GSA). (2009). *This is our country: 2008 report on the state of LGBT human rights in Serbia.* Retrieved from http://www.ilga-europe.org/home/guide/country_by_country/serbia/2008-Annual-Report-on-the-State-of-LGBT-Human-Rights-in-Serbia

Gay Straight Alliance (GSA). (2010) *Annual report on human rights status of GLBT persons in Serbia 2009.* Retrieved from http://www.ilga-europe.org/home/guide/country_by_country/serbia/Annual-Report-on-Human-Rights-Status-of-GLBT-Persons-in-Serbia-2009

Gay Straight Alliance (GSA). (2011). *Step by step. Report on human rights of LGBT persons in Serbia 2010.* Retrieved from http://en.gsa.org.rs/wp-content/uploads/2012/08/GSA-report-2010.pdf

Gay Straight Alliance (GSA). (2012). Freedom is not given, freedom is taken. Report on human rights status of LGBT persons in Serbia 2011. Retrieved from http://en.gsa.org.rs/wp-content/uploads/2012/08/GSA-report-2011.pdf

Gay Straight Alliance (GSA). (2013, October 8). Kidnapping because of the sexual orientation. Belgrade. Retrieved from http://en.gsa.org.rs/2013/10/kidnapping-because-of-the-sexual-orientation/

Gayten-LGBT, Transgender Europe, & ILGA Europe. (2013, January 18). Submission by Gayten-LGBTI, Transgender Europe2 and ILGA-Europee on the 2nd report by Serbia on the implementation of the revised European Social Charter Article 11 -- The right to protection of health. Sterilisation and other medical treatment as compulsory requirements for legal gender recognition. Comments from the Serbian LGBT Network and ILGA Europe on the 2nd Report by Serbia on the implementation of the European Social Charter (RAP/RCha/SE/2(2013). Council of Europe. Retrieved from http://www.coe.int/t/dghl/monitoring/socialcharter/reporting/statereports/CommentsILGASerbia2013_fr.pdf

Gender & Development Social Union (G&D). (2009). *Discrimination and violence against lesbians, bisexual women and transgender people in Azerbaijan Republic.* Retrieved from http://www2.ohchr.org/english/bodies/cedaw/docs/ngos/Gender_Development_Social_Union_azerbaijan_cedaw44.pdf

Gender & Development Social Union (G&D). (2009, July 20). Oral statement by Gender & Development at the Informal meeting between the CEDAW Committee and NGOs: NGO Statements. 44th CEDAW Session (20 July - 7 August 2009). Retrieved from http://www.iwraw-ap.org/resources/pdf/44_oral_statements/Azerbaijan_LBT.doc

Gender and Development Social Union (G&D). ILGA Europe, & Global Rights. (2009). *The violations of the rights of lesbian, gay, bisexual, transgender persons in Azerbaijan: a shadow report.* Submitted during the third periodic report to the UN Human Rights Committee. Retrieved from http://www2.ohchr.org/english/bodies/hrc/docs/ngos/LGBT_Azerbaijan96.pdf

GenderDoc-M. (2011a). Hate speech against LGBT people sanctioned by Moldova's law on freedom of expression. Retrieved from http://www.ilga-europe.org/home/guide/country_by_country/moldova/hate_speech_against_lgbt_people_sanctioned_by_moldova_s_law_on_freedom_of_expression

GenderDoc-M. (2011b). *Presentation of the status of Lesbian, Gay, Bisexual and Transgender Rights in the Republic of Moldova for Universal Periodic Review.* Retrieved from http://lib.ohchr.org/HRBodies/UPR/Documents/session12/MD/GENDERDOC-M-eng.pdf

GenderDoc-M. (2011c). *Report on state of human rights of LGBT people in the Republic of Moldova.* Retrieved from http://www.ilga-europe.org/home/guide/country_by_country/moldova/report_on_state_of_human_rights_of_lgbt_people_in _the_republic_of_moldova_2011

GenderDoc-M. (2012a). Overview of report outputs by GenderDoc-M, including donor finances for 2011. Retrieved from http://www.lgbt.md/eng/content.php?sid=9

GenderDoc-M. (2012b). Republic of Moldova is found liable for banning LGBT demonstration in Moldova. Retrieved from http://www.lgbt.md/eng/story.php?sid=276

GenderDoc-M. (2102c). "Try to call me a homosexual…" Letter from a former Balti city councilor's son. Lobby & Advocacy. Retrieved from http://www.lgbt.md/eng/story.php?sid=252

GenderDoc-M, Global Rights, ILGA-Europe and the International Human Rights Clinic, & Harvard Law School. (2009). *The violations of the rights of lesbian, gay, bisexual and transgender persons in Moldova: a shadow* report. Submitted to the Human Rights Committee. Retrieved from http://www.globalrights.org/site/DocServer/LGBT_ICCPR_Shadow_Report_Moldova.pdf?docID=11205

Georgian Trade Unions Confederation. (2010). PDF of extracts of Law – Unofficial English translation. Labour Code of Georgia (Law No. 4113 of 17 December 2010. Retrieved from http://www.ilo.org/dyn/natlex/docs/ELECTRONIC/88313/105780/F-353247448/GEO88313%20Eng.pdf

Gess, M. (2013, August 10). As a gay parent I must flee Russia or lose my children. Draconian new laws brand homosexuals second-class citizens in Putin's regime. *The Guardian/The Observer.* Retrieved from http://www.theguardian.com/commentisfree/2013/aug/11/anti-gay-laws-russia

Geydar L., Dovbakh A. (2007). *Being Lesbian in Ukraine: Gaining Strength.* Kiev: IEC Women's Network. Retrieved from http://www.feminist.org.ua/about/projekt/lesbian_ua2007.php

Ghilasacu, N. (2011, August 18). LGBT in Moldova: Life's not easy. *Osservatorio Balcani e Caucaso.* Rovereto, Italy: Osservatorio Balcani e Caucaso. Retrieved from http://www.balcanicaucaso.org/eng/Regions-and-countries/Moldova/LGBT-in-Moldova-life-s-not-easy-100418

Girard, F. (2008). Negotiating sexual rights and sexual orientation at the UN. Parker, R., Petchesky, R., & Sember, R. (eds.). *Sex politics: reports from the front lines* (pp.311-358). New York: Sexuality Policy Watch. Retrieved from http://www.sxpolitics.org/frontlines/book/pdf/sexpolitics.pdf

GISH. (2005). *Research and opinions on the Albanian legal situation in relation to LGBT rights.* Retrieved from http://www.ilga-europe.org/home/guide/country_by_country/albania/research_and_opinions_on_the_albanian_legial_situatio n_in_relation_to_lgbt_rights

GISH. (2006). *Survey Research with the LGBT Community in Albania.* Retrieved from http://www.ilga-europe.org/home/guide/country_by_country/albania/survey_research_with_lgbt_community_in_albania_sum mer_2006

Globa, B. (2013, October 13). The EU-Ukraine tango on gay rights. Euobserver.com Opinion. Retrieved from http://euobserver.com/opinion/121897

Global Forum on MSM & HIV. (2011). Establishment of the Eurasian Coalition on Male Health (ECOM). Retrieved from http://www.msmgf.org/index.cfm/id/11/aid/4067

Global Rights. (2008). *Demanding credibility and sustaining activism: a guide to sexuality-based advocacy.* Retrieved from http://www.globalrights.org/site/DocServer/Guide__sexuality_based_initiative.pdf?docID=10083

Global Rights, ILGA-Europe, Russian LGBT Network, FtM Phoenix Group, & Russian Transgender Fund. (2009, October). *Violations of the rights of lesbian, gay, bisexual and transgender persons in Russia. a shadow report.* Submission to the Human Rights Council. Retrieved from http://www2.ohchr.org/english/bodies/hrc/docs/ngos/JointStatement_Russia97.pdf

Global Rights, & Inclusive Foundation. (2007a). *Violations of the rights of lesbian, gay, bisexual, transgender persons in Georgia: a shadow report.* Submitted to the UN Human Rights Committee. Retrieved from http://www2.ohchr.org/english/bodies/hrc/docs/ngos/GRPJ_Georgia.pdf

Global Rights, Organization LOGOS, Organization Q. (2007b). *The status of lesbian, gay, bisexual and transgender rights in Bosnia and Herzegovina: a shadow report.* Submitted to the UN Human Rights Committee. Retrieved from http://www.globalrights.org/site/DocServer/Shadow_Report_Bosnia.pdf?docID=9903

Global Voices. (2012, May 17). Georgia: LGBT activists attacked by orthodox religious group. Retrieved from http://globalvoicesonline.org/2012/05/17/georgia-lgbt-activists-attacked-by-orthodox-religious-group/

Gorelov, D.M. (n.d.). "Status and problems of the LGBT movement in Ukraine." Analytical note. Kyiv: National Institute for Strategic Studies. Retrieved from: http://www.niss.gov.ua/articles/1206/

Gorshenin Institute. (2010, December 24). Ukrainians condemn drug use, prostitution, and suicide-survey[Russian]. Retrieved from http://institute.gorshenin.ua/news/2_ukraintsi_osuzhdayut_upotreblenie.html

Government of Georgia. (2012, April 19). Law on some changes to some legislative acts. *Legislative Herald.* Retrieved from https://matsne.gov.ge/index.php?option=com_ldmssearch&view=docView&id=1637963

Group for the Advancement of Psychiatry (GAP). (n.d.). *The history of psychiatry & homosexuality.* Retrieved from http://www.aglp.org/gap/1_history/

The Guardian. (2013, June 29). Russian police detain dozens after clashes during gay rights march. Marchers in Saint Petersburg against new anti-gay law confronted by opponents throwing eggs, flares and stones. *theguardian.com.* Retrieved from http://www.theguardian.com/world/2013/jun/29/russian-police-gay-rights

Hammarberg, T. (2009, July 29). *Human Rights and gender identity: Issue paper.* Strasbourg: Council of Europe. Retrieved from https://wcd.coe.int/ViewDoc.jsp?id=1476365

Hanisch, C. (1970). The personal is the political. Notes from the second year: Women's liberation: Major writings of the radical feminists.

Helsinki Committee for Human Rights in Serbia. (2010). *Annual report on human rights: Serbia in 2009. Europeanization—Accomplishments and limitations.* Retrieved from http://www.internal-displacement.org/8025708F004CE90B/(httpDocuments)/038D96/356879B9AC12577BB002E586C/$file/Helsinki+Committee+for+Human+Rights+in+Serbia,++Annual+report+on+human+rights+Serbia+in+2009;++Europeanization+%E2%80%93+Accomplishments+And+Limitations,+2010.pdf

Helsinki Committee for Human Rights of the Republic of Macedonia. (2011, November 29). *Annual report on the situation of human rights of LGBT people in the Republic of Macedonia in 2010.* Retrieved from http://www.ilga-europe.org/home/guide/country_by_country/fyr_macedonia/annual_report_on_the_situation_of_human_rights_of_lgbt_people_in_the_republic_of_macedonia_in_2010

Hermann, T. (2012, May 3). Pro-abortion and pro-homosexual youth lobby sent home empty-handed from UN. *Catholic Family & Human Rights Institute.* Retrieved from http://www.c-fam.org/fridayfax/volume-15/pro-abortion-and-pro-homosexual-youth-lobby-sent-home-empty-handed-from-un.html

Historia IME. (2013a, May 5). Historical for LGBT. Albania has a hate crime legislation. Historia IME. Tirana. Retrieved from http://historia-ime.com/en/english/143-historical-for-lgbt-albania-has-a-hate-crime-legislation.html

Historia IME. (2013b, May 17). Wonderful IDAHO in Albania. English. Tirana. Retrieved from http://historia-ime.com/en/english/146-wonderful-IDAHO-in-albania.html

Human Rights Action. (2009, October). Homophobia in Montenegro: public opinion poll. Retrieved from http://www.hraction.org/wp-content/uploads/homophobia-in-montenegro-presentation.pdf

Human Rights Watch. (2006). *Pride and violence: A chronicle of the events of May 27, 2006 in Moscow. [briefing paper].* Retrieved from http://www.hrw.org/legacy/backgrounder/eca/russia0606/index.htm

Human Rights Watch. (2009). *Human Rights Watch UPR submission on Albania*. Retrieved from
    http://lib.ohchr.org/HRBodies/UPR/Documents/Session6/AL/HRW_ALB_UPR_S06_2009.pdf

Human Rights Watch. (2013). *World report 2013. Events of 2012*. New York: Seven Stories Press. Retrieved from
    https://www.hrw.org/sites/default/files/wr2013_web.pdf

Icelandic Human Rights Centre. (n.d.) The right ot equality and non-discrimination. Reykjavik. Retrieved from
    http://www.humanrights.is/the-human-rights-
    project/humanrightscasesandmaterials/humanrightsconceptsideasandfora/substantivehumanrights/therighttoeq
    ualityandnondiscrimination/

ICF International. (n.d.). DHS model questionnaires. Survey types. What we do. MEASURE DHS. Calverton, MD:
    USAID. Retrieved from http://www.measuredhs.com/What-We-Do/Survey-Types/DHS-Questionnaires.cfm

ILGA. (2010) ILGA: 1978 – 2007. A chronology. ILGA. Retrieved from http://ilga.org/ilga/en/article/mG6UVpR17x

ILGA-Europe. (n.d.). Home page. Retrieved from http://www.ilga-europe.org/

ILGA-Europe. (2006). *Prides against prejudice: a toolkit for Pride organising in a hostile environment*. Retrieved from
    http://www.ilga-europe.org/home/publications/reports_and_other_materials/(offset)/15

ILGA-Europe. (2010). *CoE Recommendations. Toolkit for promoting implementation of the Recommendation at national
    level*. Retrieved from http://ilga-
    europe.org/home/guide/council_of_europe/lgbt_rights/recommendation_of_the_committee_of_ministers_o
    n_lgbt_rights

ILGA-Europe. (2011a). *Rainbow Europe Map and Index*. Retrieved from http://www.ilga-
    europe.org/home/publications/reports_and_other_materials/rainbow_map_and_index_2011_2012

ILGA-Europe. (2011b). Links page to OSCE materials. Retrieved from http://www.ilga-
    europe.org/home/issues/hate_crime/challenging_hate_crime/ilga_europe_and_osce

ILGA-Europe. (2011c, April 4). *First case from Georgia to the European Court of Human Rights concerning police
    homophobia*. Retrieved from http://www.ilga-
    europe.org/home/guide/country_by_country/georgia/first_case_from_georgia_to_the_european_court_of_h
    uman_rights_concerning_police_homophobia

ILGA-Europe. (2011d, April 29). ILGA-Europe's 2011 submissions to the European Commission: Progress reports
    on Albania, Bosnia, Kosovo, Macedonia, Montenegro and Serbia. Retrieved from http://www.ilga-
    europe.org/home/how_we_work/european_institutions/enlargement/submissions

ILGA-Europe. (2011e, August 25). Call for urgent investigation of extreme violence used by the police against a
    transgender in Tirana. Retrieved from http://www.ilga-
    europe.org/home/guide/country_by_country/albania/call_for_urgent_investigation_of_extreme_violence_use
    d_by_the_police_against_a_transgender_in_tirana#

ILGA-Europe. (2011f, September 12). *PRECIS good practice booklet*. Retrieved from http://www.ilga-
    europe.org/home/how_we_work/previous_projects/precis/booklet

ILGA-Europe. (2012a). Website portal page. ILGA-Europe trainings and study sessions on capacity building.
    Retrieved from
    http://ilga-europe.org/home/how_we_work/developing/trainings_and_seminars

ILGA-Europe. (2012b, March 5). Belarus leader: 'Better a dictator than gay.' http://www.ilga-
    europe.org/home/guide/country_by_country/belarus/belarus_leader_better_a_dictator_than_gay

ILGA-Europe. (2012c). "Homosexual propaganda" bans in Russia. Retrieved from
    http://lib.ohchr.org/HRBodies/UPR/Documents/Session16/RU/ILGA_UPR_RUS_S16_2013_ILGAEurope_E.p
    df

ILGA-Europe. (2012d). ILGA-Europe's submission to the European Commission's 2012 Progress Report on FYR Macedonia. Retreived from http://www.ilga-europe.org/home/how_we_work/european_institutions/enlargement/submissions/ilga_europe_s_submission_to_the_2012_progress_report_on_fyr_macedonia

ILGA-Europe. (2012e, March 5). Submission by the International Lesbian and Gay Association (European Region) on the 4th National Report by Ukraine on the implementation of the revised European Social Charter: Article 1.2: Prohibition of discrimination in employment on the grounds of sexual orientation and gender identity. Retrieved from http://www.coe.int/t/dghl/monitoring/socialcharter/reporting/statereports/Ukraine4CommentsNGO_en.pdf

ILGA-Europe. (2013a). FYR Macedonia annual review. Guide to Europe. Retrieved from http://www.ilga-europe.org/home/guide_europe/country_by_country/fyr_macedonia/review_2013

ILGA-Europe. (2013b). Rainbow Europe index 2013. Rainbow Europe. Brussels: Author. Retrieved from http://www.ilga-europe.org/home/publications/reports_and_other_materials/rainbow_europe

ILGA-Europe. (2013c). Rainbow Map. Explanatory Document. Author. Retrieved from http://www.ilga-europe.org/media_library/ilga_europe/publications/reports_and_other_publications/rainbow_map_2013

ILGA -Europe, COC Netherlands, the Office of Public Defender (Ombudsman) of Georgia, & Inclusive Foundation. (2011). The status of lesbian, gay, bisexual and transgender rights in Georgia. Submission to the Human Rights Council for the 10th session of Universal Periodic Review Working Group. Retrieved from http://lib.ohchr.org/HRBodies/UPR/Documents/Session10/GE/JS3_JointSubmission3-eng.pdf

Immigration and Refugee Board of Canada. (2011). Overview of Kosovar LGBT situation. Response to information request KOS103872.E. Retrieved from http://www.irb-cisr.gc.ca:8080/RIR_RDI/RIR_RDI.aspx?id=453700&l=e

Inclusive Foundation, Georgian Young Lawyers' Association & ILGA-Europe. (2008). European Social Charter: shadow report. (This report is no longer available online as Inclusive Foundation's website went out of operation in April 2012).

Informal Coalition Macedonia without Discrimination. (2011). [Stakeholder report]. Retrieved from http://lib.ohchr.org/HRBodies/UPR/Documents/Session5/MK/MWD_MKD_UPR_S5_2009_MacedoniaWithoutDiscrimination_JOINT.pdf

The Informal NGO Coalition for UPR. (2010). [Stakeholder report]. Retrieved from http://lib.ohchr.org/HRBodies/UPR/Documents/Session7/BA/Informal_UPR_Coalition_UPR_BIH_S07_2010_InfUPRCoa.pdf

Informational-Educational Center Za Ravnie Prava & Insight. (2010, January). Discrimination and violence against lesbian and bisexual women and transgender people in Ukraine. Shadow report. 45th CEDAW Session (18 January - 5 February, 2010). Retrieved from http://inclusive-foundation.org/home/files/discrimination_survey_results_en.pdf from http://www2.ohchr.org/english/bodies/cedaw/docs/Za_Ravnie_PravaandInsight-LGBT_focus_Ukraine.pdf

Institute of Church-State Relations and Law. (2007). Gay-parade as an element of the globalism of militant immorality. (English text at page 82). Retrieved from http://www.moral-law.ru/library/book_contre-gay.rtf

Intergroup on LGBT Rights (European Parliament). (2011, May 17). Montenegro: government fails to protect LGBT people from homophobic violence. Retrieved from http://www.lgbt-ep.eu/press-releases/montenegro-government-fails-to-protect-lgbt-people-from-homophobic-violence/

International Commission of Jurists (ICJ). (2007, March). The Yogyakarta Principles: principles on the application of international human rights law to sexual orientation and gender identity. Retrieved from http://www.yogyakartaprinciples.org/

The International Center for Not-for-Profit Law (ICNL). (2013). NCO law monitor: Russia. Retrieved from http://www.icnl.org/research/monitor/russia.html

International Coordinating Committee for National Human Rights Institutions (ICC). (2012). Directory of institutions – Europe. Retrieved from http://nhri.ohchr.org/EN/Contact/NHRIs/Pages/Europe.aspx

International Day Against Homophobia and Transphobia (IDAHO). (n.d.) Home page. Retrieved from http://www.dayagainsthomophobia.org/-About-IDAHO,2

International Day Against Homophobia and Transphobia (IDAHO). (2012). IDAHO Report 2012 – Albania. Retrieved from http://www.dayagainsthomophobia.org/IDAHO-REPORT-2012-ALBANIA,1646

International Labor Organization. (2012). Source and scope of regulations. Macedonia, the Former Yugoslav Republic of. Employment protection legislation database. Retrieved from http://www.ilo.org/dyn/eplex/termmain.showCountry?p_lang=en&p_country_id=42

International Planned Parenthood Federation (IPPF). (2009). Pocket guides portal. Sexual rights: an IPPF declaration. Retrieved from http://www.ippf.org/en/Resources/Statements/Sexual+rights+an+IPPF+declaration.htm

International Planned Parenthood Federation (IPPF). (2005.) *Sexual diversity tool kit.* Retrieved from http://www.ippfwhr.org/sites/default/files/files/English_SD_Tool_Kit_PDF.pdf

International Planned Parenthood Federation European Network. (2011 December). Sexuality education in Europe and Central Asia. *Choices.* Brussels: Author. Retrieved from http://www.ippfen.org/NR/rdonlyres/CAEAED62-A6D0-4327-B109-87F9B80AB501/0/ippfchoices2011.pdf

ISHR. (2011, March 24). *Ground-breaking statement on sexual orientation and gender identity by record number of 85 States.* New York: International Service for Human Rights. Retrieved from http://www.ishr.ch/council/376-council/1033-ground-breaking-statement-on-sexual-orientation-and-gender-identity-by-record-number-of-85-states

Ivantchenko, S. (2010). *Situation of transgender persons in Ukraine: research report.* Kiev. Insight NGO. Retrieved from http://insight-ukraine.org.ua/media/TRP_report.pdf (Russian), http://www.ilga-europe.org/home/guide/country_by_country/ukraine/situation_of_transgender_persons_in_ukraine (English)

Jarrow, A. (2012, June 21). The backlash. IntLawGrrls. Blog. Retrieved June 27, 2012, from http://www.intlawgrrls.com/2012/06/backlash.html

Jomarjidze, N. (2012, May 10). Georgian Laws Discriminate on Transgender Rights. CRS Issue 641. Tbilisi: Institute for War & Peace Reporting. Retrieved from http://iwpr.net/report-news/georgian-laws-discriminate-transgender-rights

Karmanau, Y. (2013, February 15). Gays in Belarus face reprisals for activism. *AP, Huffington Post.* Retrieved from http://www.huffingtonpost.com/2013/02/15/gays-in-belarus-face-repr_0_n_2697873.html

Kirichenko, K. (2011). *Situation of transsexual people in the Russian regions: Document change and access to specific health care services.* St. Petersburg: LGBT Network. http://www.lgbtnet.ru/eng/

Kochetkov, I., & Kirichenko, X. (2008). *Situation of lesbians, gays, bisexuals and transgenders in the Russian Federation.* Moscow: Moscow Helsinki Group. Retrieved from http://www.ilga-europe.org/home/guide/country_by_country/russia/situation_of_lesbians_gays_bisexuals_and_transgenders_in_the_russian_federation_2008

Kohler, W. (2012, April 6). "Gay Russian website under cyber attack after gay activist arrested for violating ban on homosexuality." *Back2Stonewall.* Retrieved May 3, 2012, from http://www.back2stonewall.com/2012/04/gay-russian-website-cyber-attack-gay-activst-arrested-violating-ban-homosexuality.html

Kravtsova, Y. (2013, January 28). We live in Russia, not Sodom and Gomorrah. *The Moscow Times.* Retrieved from http://www.themoscowtimes.com/news/article/we-live-in-russia-not-sodom-and-gomorrah/474609.html

Kreuzahler, N., Sok, E., & Zhegrova. (2012). Living openly gay in Kosovo's homophobic society. *Face the Balkans.* Retrieved from http://www.facethebalkans.com/site/semi-the-brave/

Krikorian, O. (24 May 2012). Arson attack on gay-friendly bar in Yerevan raises fears of nationalist extremism. *Ararat Magazine*. Retrieved from http://araratmagazine.org/2012/05/arson-attack-on-gay-friendly-bar-in-yerevan-raises-fears-of-nationalist-extremism/

Labris. (2009). *Annual report on the position of LGBTIQ population in Serbia for 2008*. Retrieved from http://www.labris.org.rs/en/images/stories/izvestaji/izvestaj_2008_EN.pdf

Labris. (2010). *Annual report on the position of LGBTIQ population in Serbia for 2009*. Retrieved from http://www.labris.org.rs/en/images/stories/izvestaji/izvestajEN.pdf

Labris and Gayten-LGBT. (2012). The Universal Periodic Review. Belgrade. Retrieved from http://lib.ohchr.org/HRBodies/UPR/Documents/Session15/RS/JS4_UPR_S15_JointSubmission4_E.pdf

Labrys. (2008). Labrys writes reports on sexual and reproductive rights in Azerbaijan, Turkmenistan and Uzbekistan. Lesbian, bisexual and Transgender Organization in Kyrgyzstan. Retrieved from http://kyrgyzlabrys.wordpress.com/2008/09/10/labrys-writes-reports-on-sexual-and-reproductive-rights-in-azerbaijan-turkmenistan-and-uzbekistan/

Lally, K. (2013, September 29). Russia anti-gay law casts a shadow over Sochi's 2014 Olympics. The *Washington Post*. Retrieved from http://articles.washingtonpost.com/2013-09-29/world/42510859_1_sochi-russia-anti-gay-law-olympic-boycott

Levy, M. (2007, May 27). Eggs and punches at Russia gay march. *BBC News*. Retrieved from http://news.bbc.co.uk/2/hi/europe/6696329.stm

LGBT Forum Progress. (2012, March 15). The State is now financing gender reassignment procedures for transgender persons [Press release]. Retrieved from http://lgbtprogres.me/en/2012/03/zna%C4%8Dajan-doga%C4%91aj-za-transrodnu-zajednicu/

LGBT Forum Progress. (2013, April 10), The first change of the personal name successfully completed—Amendment act of identity cards initiated. Retrieved from http://lgbtprogres.me/en/2013/04/1832/

LGBT Human Rights Nash Mir Center. (2013a). *Hate crimes against LGBT persons in Ukraine over 2012-2013*. English summary of the report. Kyiv. Retrieved from http://www.gay.org.ua/publications/hate_crime_2013-e.pdf

LGBT Human Rights Nash Mir Center. (2013a). Re: Situation of LGBT in Ukraine in 2013[memo].

LGBT Human Rights Project GayBelarus.By. (2009). *The status of Lesbian, Gay, Bisexual and Transgender Rights in the Republic of Belarus*. Retrieved from http://lib.ohchr.org/HRBodies/UPR/Documents/Session8/BY/GayBelarus_UPR_BLR_S08_2010_GayBelarus.pdf

LGBT Network. (2012). *The Universal Periodic Review*. St. Petersburg. Retrieved from http://lib.ohchr.org/HRBodies/UPR/Documents/Session16/RU/LGBTNET_UPR_RUS_S16_2013_LGBTNetwork_E.pdf

LGBT United Macedonia. (2013). Skopje pride. *ILGA Europe*. Retrieved from http://www.ilga-europe.org/home/guide_europe/country_by_country/fyr_macedonia/skopje_pride

Lokshina, T. (2012, April 26). Russia: Is wearing a pink triangle a crime? *Global Post*. Retrieved from http://www.globalpost.com/dispatches/globalpost-blogs/commentary/russia-wearing-pink-triangle-crime

Loudes, C. & Paradis, E. (2008) *Handbook on monitoring and reporting homophobic and transphobic incidents*. Brussels: ILGA-Europe. Retrieved from http://www.ilga-europe.org/home/publications/reports_and_other_materials/(offset)/15

Lowder, J. (2012, December 3). Being transgender is no longer a disorder: The American Psychiatric Association salutes the T in LGBT. *Slate*. Retrieved from http://www.slate.com/articles/health_and_science/medical_examiner/2012/12/dsm_revision_and_sexual_identity_gender_identity_disorder_replaced_by_gender.html

Macedonian Association for Free Sexual Orientation (MASSO), Global Rights, ILGA-Europe. (2008, March). Violations of the rights of lesbian, gay, bisexual, transgender persons in the former Yugoslav Republic of Macedonia: a shadow report. Submission to the Human Rights Council. Retrieved from http://www.globalrights.org/site/DocServer/Shadow_Report_Macedonia.pdf

Martirosyan, S. (2013, September 20). The 'Gender equality law' hysteria in Armenia. The Armenian Weekly featured headline special report. Retrieved from http://www.armenianweekly.com/2013/09/20/the-gender-equality-law-hysteria-in-armenia/

Media Diversity Institute (MDI). (2006, April). *Media Coverage of Minority Groups in the South Caucasus 2004 – 2006.* Retrieved from www.rhiz.eu/download.php?id=2514

Milosevice, M. (2013, October 21). Montenegro details 60 after gay pride march. BalkanInsight. Retreived from http://www.balkaninsight.com/en/article/montenegro-detains-60-after-gay-parade

Milosevic, S. (2012, May 30). Serbia: For gays, a ghetto in modern Europe. *Global Post.* Retrieved from http://www.globalpost.com/dispatch/news/culture-lifestyle/111221/serbia-gays-ghetto-modern-europe

Mobasherat. M. (2011, May 28). Dozens arrested in Moscow gay rights parade clashes. *CNN Europe.* Retrieved from http://edition.cnn.com/2011/WORLD/europe/05/28/russia.gay.rights.parade.clashes/

Muradyan, A. (2013 August, 13). Storm over "Gender" word in Armenia. Report News Caucasus. Institute for War & Peace Reporting. Retrieved from http://iwpr.net/report-news/crs-issue-697

Napikoski, L. (n.d.). Women's history: the personal is political. *About.com.* Retrieved from http://womenshistory.about.com/od/feminism/a/consciousness_raising.htm

Nash Mir Gay and Lesbian Centre. (2005). *Gay rights are human rights: report about discrimination on the grounds of sexual orientation in Ukraine.* Retrieved from http://www.ilga-europe.org/home/guide/country_by_country/ukraine/gay_rights_are_human_rights

Nash Mir Gay and Lesbian Centre. (2007). Ukrainian homosexuals & society: A reciprocation. *Review of the situation: society, authorities and politicians, mass-media, legal issues, gay-community.* Kyiv: Author. Retrieved from http://lib.ohchr.org/HRBodies/UPR/Documents/Session2/UA/NM_UKR_UPR_S2_2008_NashMirGayandLesbianCenter_urpsubmission.pdf

Nash Mir Gay and Lesbian Centre. (2011). *Public opinion about homosexuals in Ukraine: review of the sociological research.* Retrieved from http://www.gay.org.ua/publications/society2011brief-e.doc

Nash Mir Gay and Lesbian Centre. (2013). *LGBT vector of Ukraine. The situation of LGBT in Ukraine (November 2011-2012).* Kyiv: Nash Mir, Council of LGBT Organisations in Ukraine, Royal Netherlands Embassy in Kyiv, Remembrance, Responsibility and Future Foundation. Retrieved from http://www.gay.org.ua/publications/lgbt_ukraine_2012-e.pdf

National Statistical Service [Armenia], Ministry of Health [Armenia], and ICF International. (2012). *Armenia Demographic and Health Survey 2010.* Calverton, Maryland: USAID, UNICEF, UNFPA & UNAIDS. Retrieved from http://www.measuredhs.com/publications/publication-FR252-DHS-Final-Reports.cfm

Natsvlishvili, A. & Aghdgomelashvili, E. (2012). *LBT women in Georgia: shadow report.* Submitted to the Committee on the Elimination of all Forms of Discrimination against Women (CEDAW). Tbilisi: Women's Initiative Supporting Group (WISG). Retrieved from http://women.ge/wp-content/uploads/2012/05/WISG-LBT-CEDAW-shadow-report_eng.pdf

Netherlands Institute for Human Rights (NIHR). (2010, October 21). Alekseyev v. Russia (judgment). Retrieved from http://sim.law.uu.nl/sim/caselaw/Hof.nsf/1d4d0dd240bfee7ec12568490035df05/0aba6ec1928c4036c12577c2002e6fc3?OpenDocument

New Kaliningrad. (2013, January 24). Oblast Duma prohibited propaganda of homoseuualism and pedophilia in the region. News, Politics. Retrieved from http://www.newkaliningrad.ru/news/politics/1819502-oblduma-zapretila-propagandu-gomoseksualizma-i-pedofilii-v-regione.html

Office of the High Commissioner for Human Rights (OHCHR). (2001). *Professional training series no. 7: training manual on human rights monitoring.* Geneva: United Nations. Retrieved from http://www.ohchr.org/Documents/Publications/training7Introen.pdf

Office of the High Commissioner for Human Rights (OHCHR). (2009). Digital record of the UDHR. Retrieved from http://www.ohchr.org/EN/NEWSEVENTS/Pages/DigitalrecordoftheUDHR.aspx

Office of the High Commissioner for Human Rights (OHCHR). (2010). *National human rights institutions. History, principles, roles and responsibilities.* Geneva: United Nations. Retrieved from http://www.ohchr.org/Documents/Publications/PTS-4Rev1-NHRI_en.pdf

Office of the High Commissioner for Human Rights (OHCHR). (2012, March 7). *Human Rights Council holds panel discussion on discrimination and violence based on sexual orientation and gender identity.* Retrieved from http://www.ohchr.org/en/NewsEvents/Pages/DisplayNews.aspx?NewsID=11920&LangID=E

Office of the High Commissioner for Human Rights (OHCHR). (2013). Combatting discrimination based on sexual orientation and gender identity. Your human rights, discrimination. Retrieved from http://www.ohchr.org/EN/Issues/Discrimination/Pages/LGBT.aspx

Office of the Press Secretary. (2011, December 6). International Initiatives to Advance the Human Rights of Lesbian, Gay, Bisexual, and Transgender Persons. Presidential Memorandum. Washington, D.C.: The White House. Retrieved from http://www.whitehouse.gov/the-press-office/2011/12/06/presidential-memorandum-international-initiatives-advance-human-rights-l

Office of the Spokesperson. (2011, December 6). *The Department of State's Accomplishments Promoting the Human Rights of Lesbian, Gay, Bisexual and Transgender People.* Factsheet. Washington, D.C.: U.S. Department of State. Retrieved from http://www.state.gov/r/pa/prs/ps/2011/12/178341.htm

Organization for Security and Cooperation in Europe (OSCE). (n.d.a).TANDIS (Tolerance information system). OSCE Office for Democratic Institutions and Human Rights. Retrieved from http://www.osce.org/odihr/44066

Organization for Security and Cooperation in Europe (OSCE). (n.d.b). Tolerance and discrimination. What we do. Retrieved from http://www.osce.org/what/tolerance

Organization for Security and Cooperation in Europe (OSCE). (n.d.c). Who we are. Home. Retrieved from http://www.osce.org/who

Organization for Security and Cooperation in Europe (OSCE). (2009). *Hate Crime Laws: A Practical Guide.* Warsaw: Office for Democratic Institutions and Human Rights. http://www.osce.org/odihr/36426

Organization for Security and Cooperation in Europe (OSCE) Office of Democratic Institutions and Human Rights (ODIHR). (n.d.a). Homophobia. Tolerance and Non-Discrimination Information System. Retrieved from http://tandis.odihr.pl/?p=home

Organization for Security and Cooperation in Europe Office of Democratic Institutions and Human Rights (OSCE/ODIHR). (n.d.b). Montenegro. Anti-discrimination. Legislation online. http://www.legislationline.org/topics/country/57/topic/84

Organization for Security and Cooperation in Europe Office of Democratic Institutions and Human Rights (OSCE/ODIHR). (2013). Constitutions. Legislationline. Retrieved from http://legislationline.org/documents/section/constitutions

Organization Q. (2008). *Queer Sarajevo Festival: Narrative report.* Retrieved from http://www.ilga-europe.org/home/guide/country_by_country/bosnia_herzegovina/report_by_q_on_queer_sarajevo_festival_2008

Organization Q and the Sexual Rights Initiative. (2010). Report on Bosnia and Herzegovina 7th round of the Universal Periodic Review – February 2010. Retrieved from http://lib.ohchr.org/HRBodies/UPR/Documents/Session7/BA/JS_UPR_BIH_S07_2010_JointSubmission.pdf

Orrick, Herrington & Sutcliffe LLP. (2009). Serbia national discrimination laws. Equal Rights Trust. Retrieved from http://www.equalrightstrust.org/ertdocumentbank/395178321_5__PILI%20Project%20-%20Serbia%20Summary%20Template%20for%20National%20Law.pdf

Ottosson, D. (2006). *LGBT world legal wrap up survey*. Brussels: International Lesbian and Gay Association. Retrieved from http://www.gaylawnet.com/ezine/crime/ilga_nov08.pdf

Parliamentary Assembly of Bosnia and Herzegovina- House of Representatives. (2009). Law on prohibition of discrimination [English translation]. Sarajevo: Organization Q. http://www.queer.ba/en/content/law-prohibition-discrimination

Parliamentary Assembly of Bosnia and Herzegovina. (2010). Law on gender equality in Bosnia and Herzegovina. Gender Equality Agency of Bosnia and Herzegovina. Retrieved from http://www.arsbih.gov.ba/en/legal-framework/law-on-gender-equality-in-bih

Peers, S. (2011, October). *The legal grounds for inclusive EU legislation against bias, violence and hatred.* Brussels: ILGA-Europe. Retrieved from http://www.ilga-europe.org/home/publications/reports_and_other_materials/research_legal_grounds_2011

Pink Armenia. (2013). *Monitoring of human rights violations of LGBT people in Armenia.* Retrieved from http://issuu.com/pinkarmenia/docs/lgbtmonitoring/1?e=4137256/5170316

Pink Armenia. (2011a). *LGBT rights situation in Armenia 2011* (summary). Retrieved from http://www.pinkarmenia.org/en/2012/02/lgbtreport2011/

Pink Armenia. (2011b, June 13). Historic memorandum between Armenia human rights Ombudsman and PINK Armenia on protection of LGBT rights. *PINK Armenia blogspot.* Retrieved from http://pinkarmenia.blogspot.com/2011/06/historic-memorandum-between-armenia.html

Pink Armenia. (2011c). *We are our rights: public attitude toward LGBT persons in Yerevan, Gyumri and Vanadzor: 2011.* Retrieved from http://www.pinkarmenia.org/publication/lgbtsurveyen.pdf

Pink Armenia. (2011d). Shadow report: Human rights violations fo LGBT people in Armenia. Retrieved from http://www.pinkarmenia.org/en/2013/03/lgbtshadowreport/

Pink Embassy. (2012, December 24). Discriminatory texts should be changed or removed from circulation. Domestic news. Retrieved from http://www.pinkembassy.al/en/node/489

Pink Embassy. (2011, September). *Report into human rights violations of the LGBT community in Albania: May 2010 – May 2011.* Retrieved from http://www.ilga-europe.org/home/guide/country_by_country/albania/REPORT-INTO-HUMAN-RIGHTS-VIOLATIONS-OF-THE-LGBT-COMMUNITY-IN-ALBANIA

Pink News. (2012a, March 27). *Serbia: Far-right leader jailed for homophobic death-threats.* Retrieved from http://www.pinknews.co.uk/2012/03/27/serbia-far-right-leader-jailed-for-homophobic-death-threats/

Pink News. (2012b, April 24). *Straight Russian man cleared of 'gay propaganda' charge in St Petersburg.* Retrieved from http://www.pinknews.co.uk/2012/04/24/straight-russian-man-cleared-of-gay-propaganda-charge-in-st-petersburg/

Pink News. (2012c, April 25). *Russia: Father imprisoned gay teen son in rehab clinic after a witch failed to exorcise his homosexuality.* Retrieved from http://www.pinknews.co.uk/2012/04/25/russia-father-imprisoned-gay-teen-son-in-rehab-clinic-after-a-witch-failed-to-exorcise-his-homosexuality/

Plotka, M. (2013, March 12). *Fear of the other. The problem of homophobia in Russia[in Russian].* Moscow: Levada Center. Retrieved from http://www.levada.ru/12-03-2013/strakh-drugogo-problema-gomofobii-v-rossii

Polácek, R. & Le Déroff, J. (2010, September). Joining forces to combat homophobic and transphobic hate crime: cooperation between police forces and LGBT organisations in Europe. Brussels: ILGA-Europe. Retrieved from http://www.ilga-europe.org/home/publications/reports_and_other_materials

Polácek, R. & Le Déroff, J. (2011, October). ILGA-Europe toolkit for training police officers on tackling LGBTI-phobic crime ILGA-Europe Toolkit for training police officers on tackling LGBTI-phobic crime. Brussels: ILGA-Europe. Retrieved from http://www.ilga-europe.org/home/publications/reports_and_other_materials/training_toolkit_police_2011

Public Opinion Foundation. (2006). Sexual minorities. The Ban on holding a gay parade[in Russian]. Retrieved from http://bd.fom.ru/report/map/dd062227

Quinn, S. (2007). *Forced out: LGBT people in Georgia.* Brussels: International Lesbian and Gay Association – European Region. Retrieved from http://www.ilga-europe.org/content/download/9372/55934/file/georgia.pdf

Radio Free Europe. (2012, April 30). *Activists predict rise in gay asylum claims amid 'propaganda' ban.* Retrieved from http://www.rferl.org/content/russia_gay_rights_lgbt_asylum/24564738.html

Radio Free Europe/Radio Liberty. (2013a, October 11) Moldova rejects 'Gay propaganda' law. Retrieved from http://www.rferl.org/content/article/25134267.html

Radio Free Europe/Radio Liberty. (2013b, May 13). Ukraine MPs postpone antidiscrimination debate after protests. Retrieved from http://www.rferl.org/content/ukraine-discrimination-law-parliament/24985506.html

Radio Free Europe/Radio Liberty's (RFE/RL's) Moldovan Service. (2013, March 1). Moldovan court overturns local ban on 'gay propaganda.' *Radio Free Europe/Radio Liberty.* Retrieved from http://www.rferl.org/content/moldova-gay-propaganda-ban/24916293.html

Radoman, J., Radoman, M., Djurkjevic-Lukic, S., & Andjelkovic. (2011). *LGBT people and security sector reform in the Republic of Serbia.* Belgrade: OSCE & Public Policy Research Centre. Retrieved from http://publicpolicy.rs/wp-content/uploads/2011/12/LGBT-people-and-security-sector-reform.pdf

Regional Center for Minorities, International Human Rights Clinic – Harvard Law School and Heartland Alliance for Human Needs and Human Rights. (2010, March). *The violations of the rights of lesbian, gay, bisexual, and transgender individuals in Serbia: a shadow report.* Submitted to the Human Rights Council. Retrieved from http://www.boell.de/downloads/LGBT_ICCPR_Shadow_Report_Serbia.pdf

Reporters without Borders. (n.d.). *Press Freedom Index 2011-2012.* Retrieved April 20, 2012, from http://en.rsf.org/press-freedom-index-2011-2012,1043.html

Republic of Bashkortostan. (2012, June 25). Law of the Republic of Bashkortostan on amending the law of the Republic of Bashkortostan "On basic guarantees of the rights of the child in the Republic of Bashkortostan." Official internet-portal for legal information. Retrieved from http://www.npa.bashkortostan.ru/?show=1&seed=1176

Republic of Serbia. (2012 December 24). Act of 24 December 2012 to amend and supplement the Penal Code. Retrieved from http://www.parlament.rs/upload/archive/files/lat/pdf/zakoni/2012/4108-12Lat.pdf

RIA Novosti. (2013 May 15). Moscow says no to May 25 gay pride parade. Russia. RIANovosti. Retrieved from http://en.rian.ru/russia/20130515/181167995.html

Roller, E. (2013 June 29). Russian police arrest protesters for violating "gay propaganda" law. The Slatest. Slate. Retrieved from http://www.slate.com/blogs/the_slatest/2013/06/29/gay_pride_st_petersburg_rally_ends_in_arrests_over_gay_propaganda_law.html

Roudik, P. (2012). Moldova: Various forms of discrimination are banned by law. Washington, D.C.: Library of Congress. Retrieved from http://www.loc.gov/lawweb/servlet/lloc_news?disp3_l205403410_text

Russia Today. (2012, March, 4). 'I'd rather be a dictator than gay': Lukashenko to German FM. News. Retrieved from http://rt.com/news/lukashenko-gay-german-minister-807/

Russian Gazette. (2013, July 2). Federal law of the Russian Federation dated June 29, 2013 N-135-FZ Moscow. Moscow. Retrieved from http://www.rg.ru/2013/06/30/deti-site-dok.html

Russian LGBT Network. (2010). Submission to the CEDAW Committee. *Discrimination and violence against lesbian, bisexual and transgender people in Russia: a shadow report.* Retrieved from http://www2.ohchr.org/english/bodies/cedaw/docs/ngos/LGBTNetwork_RussianFederation46.pdf

Russian LGBT Network. (2011). Discrimination on grounds of sexual orientation and gender identity in health care, education, employment and social security in the Russian Federation: an alternative report. Submitted for the 46th CESCR Session. Retrieved from http://www2.ohchr.org/english/bodies/cescr/docs/ngos/IRSM_RussianFederation_CESCR46_en.pdf

Russian LGBT Network. (2013). The *Situation of LGBT in the Russian Federation (Last Three Months 2011 – First Half 2012).* Retrieved from: http://www.lgbtnet.ru/en/content/situation-lgbt-russian-federation-last-three-months-2011-first-half-2012

Russian Public Opinion Research Foundation. (2005, February 15). The attitudes of Russians toward homosexuals: It is early to allow single sex marriage [in Russian] [Press release]. Retrieved from http://wciom.ru/index.php?id=459&uid=1084

Sanders, D. (2011, December 17). What preceded Hillary Clinton's UN speech? *LGBT Asylum News.* Sequi, Retrieved from http://madikazemi.blogspot.com/2011/12/what-preceded-hillary-clintons-un.html

Savić, M. (2013). Invisible LGBT. Report on the position of LGBT community in Kosovo. Belgrade: Heartefact Fund. Retrieved from http://heartefact.org/wp-content/uploads/2013/02/HF.Kosovo-Report_FNL.20130125_Marija-Savic.pdf

Schilt, K. & Westbrook, L. (2009). "Doing gender, doing heteronormativity: 'Gender normals,' transgender people, and the social maintenance of heterosexuality". Gender & Society 23 (4): 440–464 [461]. doi:10.1177/0891243209340034.

Sequi, Ambassador. (2103, May 16). Speech of Ambassador Sequi to the Round table: Albania against homophobia: LGBT in front of politics, media, youth and anti-discrimination measures. Delegation of the European Union to Albania. Retrieved from http://eeas.europa.eu/delegations/albania/press_corner/all_news/news/2013/20130516_en.htm

Sexual Rights Initiative. (2008). *Report on Montenegro–3rd round of the Universal periodic Review—December 2008.* Retrieved from http://lib.ohchr.org/HRBodies/UPR/Documents/Session3/ME/SRI_MNE_UPR_S3_2008_TheSexualRightsInitiative_uprsubmission.pdf

Shabani, A. (2013, January 17). Kosovo human rights activists resist attacks on LGBT community. *Women's Media Center.* Retrieved from http://www.womensmediacenter.com/feature/entry/kosovo-human-rights-activists-resist-attacks-on-lgbt-community

Sindelar, D. (2013, April 9). Bucking the trend, Moldova emerging as regional leader in LGBT rights. *Radio Free Europe Radio Liberty.* Retrieved from http://www.rferl.org/content/moldova-lgbt-rights/24952566.html

Society for Threatened Peoples. (2012). Serbia. The situation of minorities in Serbia. Germany. Retrieved from http://lib.ohchr.org/HRBodies/UPR/Documents/Session15/RS/STP_UPR_SRB_S15_SocietyforThreatenedPeoples_E.pdf

Somach, S. (2011, July). *The other side of the gender equation: gender issues for men in the Europe and Eurasia region.* Washington, D.C.: USAID & JBS International. Retrieved from http://socialtransitions.kdid.org/sites/socialtransitions/files/resource/files/Gender_Issues_Men_7-28-11-Final.pdf

Somach, S. (2012). Domestic violence in Europe and Eurasia—2012 update. Washington, D.C.: USAID & JBS International. Retrieved from http://socialtransitions.kdid.org/sites/socialtransitions/files/resource/files/Domestic%20Violence%20Update_final_12Aug31.pdf

Soros Foundation-Moldova. (2011, January). *Perceptions of the Population of the Republic of Moldova on Discrimination: Sociological Study.* Chisinau: Soros Foundation-Moldova. Retrieved from http://www.soros.md/files/publications/documents/Studiu_sociologic_EN.pdf

Stakic, Isidora. (2011). Public discourse: How nationalist myths and stereotypes influence prejudices against the LGBT minority. *Equal Rights Review, 7.* Retrieved from http://www.equalrightstrust.org/ertdocumentbank/ERR7_isidora.pdf

Steinberg, D. (2011, June 27). Remarks by Deputy Ambassador for USAID by Don Steinberg. Panel Discussion on LGBT Issues in Foreign Policy at the U.S. Department of State. *Humanrights.gov.* Retrieved from http://www.humanrights.gov/2011/06/30/panel-discussion-on-lgbt-issues-in-foreign-policy/

Stern, D. (2012, October 11). Ukraine takes aim against 'gay propaganda.' *BBC News Magazine.* Retrieved from http://www.bbc.co.uk/news/magazine-19881905

Stojneto. (2012, July 10). Small LGBT pride in Macedonia. *CNN iReport.* Retrieved from http://ireport.cnn.com/docs/DOC-813337

Stopera, M. (2013, July 22). 36 photos from Russia that everyone needs to see. Buzzfeed LGBT. Retreived from http://www.buzzfeed.com/mjs538/photos-from-russia-everyone-needs-to-see

Tanner, A. (2010). Gay rights march in Belgrade triggers violence riots. *Reuters.* Retrieved from http://www.reuters.com/article/2010/10/10/us-serbia-gays-idUSTRE6990SP20101010

Task Force on Gender Identity and Gender Variance. (2009). *Report of the APA Task Force on Gender Identity and Gender Variance.* Washington, D.C.: American Psychological Association. Retrieved from http://www.apa.org/pi/lgbt/resources/policy/gender-identity-report.pdf

UKGayNews. (2008, May 11). *Moldovan Police Stand Accused of Letting Protestors Highjack Bus Carrying Gay Pride Participants.* Retrieved from http://ukgaynews.org.uk/Archive/08/May/1101.htm

Ukrainian Parliament Commissioner for Human Rights. (2013). Annual Report of the Verkhovna Rada of Ukraine on human rights and freedom of people and citizens. Kyiv: Author. Retrieved from http://www.ombudsman.gov.ua/images/stories/062013/Dopovid_062013.pdf

UNAIDS. (2011, October). *UNAIDS Terminology Guidelines.* Geneva: UN. Retrieved from http://www.unaids.org:80/en/media/unaids/contentassets/documents/unaidspublication/2011/JC2118_terminology-guidelines_en.pdf

UN Commission on Population and Development. (2012). Forty-fifth session. Geneva: UN. Retrieved from http://www.un.org/esa/population/cpd/cpd2012/cpd45.htm

UN Commission on Population and Development. (2012). *Report on the forty-fifth session (15 April 2011 and 23-27 April 2012).* Geneva: UN. Retrieved from http://daccess-dds-ny.un.org/doc/UNDOC/GEN/N12/337/17/PDF/N1233717.pdf?OpenElement

UNDP. (n.d.). *Human Development Reports.* UNDP. Retrieved April 20, 2012 from http://hdr.undp.org/en/statistics/

UN General Assembly. (2011) A/HRC/17/19. Human Rights Council Seventeenth session, agenda item 8. Follow-up and implementation of the Vienna Declaration and Programme of action. Resolution adopted by the Human Rights Council. 17/19 Human rights, sexual orientation and gender identity. Geneva: Human Rights Council. Retrieved from http://daccess-dds-ny.un.org/doc/UNDOC/GEN/G11/148/76/PDF/G1114876.pdf?OpenElement

United States Agency for International Development (USAID). (n.d.). LGBT in the Field. IDEA Office of Innovation & Development Alliances. Washington, D.C.: USAID. Retrieved from http://idea.usaid.gov/gp/lgbt-field

United States Agency for International Development (USAID). (2010). *Guide to gender integration and analysis: Additional help for ADS chapters 201 and 203.* Washington, DC. Retrieved from http://pdf.usaid.gov/pdf_docs/PDACP506.pdf

United States Agency for International Development (USAID). (2011a, January). *Learning from experience: USAID evaluation policy.* Washington DC. Retrieved from http://www.usaid.gov/evaluation/policy

United States Agency for International Development (USAID). (2011b). *USAID policy framework 2011-2015.* Washington, D.C. Retrieved from http://transition.usaid.gov/policy/USAID_PolicyFramework.PDF

United States Agency for International Development (USAID). (2012a, March). *Gender equality and female empowerment policy.* Washington DC. Retrieved from http://pdf.usaid.gov/pdf_docs/pdact200.pdf

United States Agency for International Development (USAID). (2012b). USAID's global health strategic framework. Better health for development 2011-2016. Washington, D.C. Retrieved from http://reliefweb.int/sites/reliefweb.int/files/resources/Full_Report_3837.pdf

United States Agency for International Development (USAID). (2013). USAID strategy on democracy human rights and governance. Washington, D.C. Retrieved from http://www.usaid.gov/sites/default/files/documents/1866/USAID%20DRG_%20final%20final%206-24%203%20(1).pdf

U.S. Department of Health and Human Services (HHS). (2011, June 29). Affordable Care Act to improve data collection, reduce health disparities. Washington, D.C.: Author. Retrieved from http://www.hhs.gov/news/press/2011pres/06/20110629a.html

U.S. Department of State. (2008). Belarus. 2007 country reports on human rights practices, Europe and Eurasia. Washington, D.C.: Author. Retrieved from http://www.state.gov/j/drl/rls/hrrpt/2007/100549.htm

U.S. Department of State. (2011). *2010 country reports on human rights practices.* Washington DC: Author. Retrieved from http://www.state.gov/j/drl/rls/hrrpt/2010/index.htm

U.S. Department of State. (2012). *2011 country reports on human rights practices.* Washington DC. Retrieved from http://www.state.gov/j/drl/rls/hrrpt/2011/index.htm

U.S. Mission to OSCE. (2010, October 27). *LGBT activists at the OSCE Review Conference, Warsaw, 2010 [interviews].* Video retrieved from http://www.youtube.com/watch?v=Q96Bo9fGvoM

Ushahidi.com. (2013). Deployments. Ushahidi Community. Retrieved from http://community.ushahidi.com/deployments/

van der Veur, D. (2007). *Forced Out: LGBT People in Azerbaijan.* Brussels: International Lesbian and Gay Association – European Region. Retrieved from http://www.ilga-europe.org/content/download/9371/55930/version/2/.../azerb.pdf

Venice Commission. (2013, June 18). Opinion 707/2012. Opinion on the issue of the prohibition of so-called "propagands of homosexuality" in the light of recent legislation in some member states of the Council of Europe. Strasbourg: Council of Europe. Retrieved from http://www.venice.coe.int/webforms/documents/?pdf=CDL-AD(2013)022-e

Verkhovna Rada of Ukraine. (2013). Draft law on amendments to certain legislative acts of Ukraine on preventing and combatting discrimination in Ukraine. Offical web portal. Retrieved from http://w1.c1.rada.gov.ua/pls/zweb2/webproc4_1?pf3511=45813

Vukovic, D., Colovic, I., & Mojsilovic, M. (2008). *Prejudices exposed—Homophobia in Serbia. Public opinion research report on LGBT population.* Belgrade: Gay Straight Alliance. Retrieved from http://gsa.org.rs/wp-content/uploads/2012/04/Research-Prejudices-Exposed-2008-GSA.pdf

Waaldijk, K. (2009). Legal recognition of homosexual orientation in the countries of the world. A chronological overview with footnotes. The Netherlands: Leiden Law School. Retrieved from https://openaccess.leidenuniv.nl/bitstream/handle/1887/14543/Waaldijk+2009+-+Legal+Recogniton+of+Homosexual+Orientation+-+Chronological+Overview.pdf;jsessionid=FC760401E023A9CDAFE80C8CBDDDA258?sequence=1

Washington, J. & Evans, N.J. (1991). Becoming an Ally. In N.J. Evans & V.A. Wall, *Beyond Tolerance: Gays, Lesbians and Bisexuals on Campus*. Alexandria, VA: American Association for Counseling and Development.

Weber, A. (2009). *Manual on hate speech*. Strasbourg, France: Council of Europe Publishing. Retrieved from http://book.coe.int/ftp/3342.pdf

Women's Initiative Supporting Group (WISG). (2011, November 17). Joint Statement of non-profit organizations "Identoba" and "Women's' Initiatives Support Group" – On the commemoration of the International Day of Tolerance [Press release]. Retrieved from http://women.ge/en/2011/11/17/statement/

Women's Initiatives Supporting Group (WISG). (2012). *Situation of LGBT Persons in Georgia*. Tbilisi: IGLA Europe, Heinrich Boell Foundation. Retrieved from http://women.ge/wp-content/uploads/2012/12/WISG_situation-of-lgbt-persons-in-Georgia_ENG-www.pdf

Wockner, R. (2008, May 22). Moldovan pride parade thwarted by violent mob. *Bay Times*. Retrieved from http://www.sfbaytimes.com/index.php?sec=article&article_id=8182

World Health Organization (WHO). (n.d.). *The ICD-10: Classification of mental and behavioral disorders; clinical descriptions and diagnostic guidelines*. Retrieved from http://www.who.int/classifications/icd/en/bluebook.pdf

Y-PEER. (n.d.) About Y-PEER. *Y-PEER*. Retrieved from http://www.ypeerinaction.org/index.php?option=com_content&view=article&id=1&Itemid=2

Zapata, J.P. (2012, March 16). Montenegro champions new law for gender reassignment. National healthcare now covers sex change procedures. *GaySTAR News*. Retrieved from http://www.gaystarnews.com/article/montenegro-champions-new-law-gender-reassignment160312

Zinchenkov, A., Kacyanchuk, M., Kravchuk, A., Maimulahin, A., Ostalenko, A., & Sheremet, C. (2011a). *One step forward, two steps back: situation of LGBT in Ukraine in 2010-2011*. Retrieved from http://www.gay.org.ua/publications/report2011-r.pdf [Ukrainian full report], http://www.hirschfeld-eddy-stiftung.de/fileadmin/images/laenderberichte/Ukraine_report2011-e.pdf [English summary report]

Zuvela, M. (2013, July 24). Violence mars first gay parade in Montenegro. Reuters. Retreived from http://www.reuters.com/article/2013/07/24/us-montenegro-gay-idUSBRE96N0HX20130724